D0832184

HOPE IN AN AGE
OF DESPAIR

HOPE IN AN AGE OF DESPAIR

And Other Talks and Writings

Albert Nolan

Edited and introduced by Stan Muyebe

ORBIS BOOKS
Maryknoll, New York 10545

Founded in 1970, Orbis Books endeavors to publish works that enlighten the mind, nourish the spirit, and challenge the conscience. The publishing arm of the Maryknoll Fathers and Brothers, Orbis seeks to explore the global dimensions of the Christian faith and mission, to invite dialogue with diverse cultures and religious traditions, and to serve the cause of reconciliation and peace. The books published reflect the views of their authors and do not represent the official position of the Maryknoll Society. To learn more about Maryknoll and Orbis Books, please visit our website at www.maryknollsociety.org.

Copyright © 2009 by Albert Nolan.

Published by Orbis Books, Maryknoll, NY 10545-0302. All rights reserved.

No part of this publication may be reproduced or transmitted in any form or by any means, electronic or mechanical, including photocopying, recording, or any information storage or retrieval system, without prior permission in writing from the publisher.

Queries regarding rights and permissions should be addressed to: Orbis Books, P.O. Box 302, Maryknoll, NY 10545-0302.

Manufactured in the United States of America

Library of Congress Cataloging-in-Publication Data

Nolan, Albert, 1934-
   Hope in an age of despair : and other writings / Albert Nolan ; edited and introduced by Stan Muyebe.
       p. cm.
   Expanded version of a lecture that was delivered on Nov. 15, 2008 on the occasion of the author receiving from the Dominican Order the title of STM (Master in Sacred Theology).
   Includes bibliographical references.
   ISBN 978-1-57075-835-5 (pbk.)
   1. Hope—Religious aspects—Christianity.   2. Church and social problems.
3. Christianity and culture.   I. Muyebe, Stanslaus C.   II. Title.
   BV4638.N65 2009
   234'.25—dc22
                                                        2009013848

Contents

Preface

I do not know how to express my thanks to my Dominican confrere, Stan Muyebe, for reading through all the bits and pieces of my writings and talks covering a period of some twenty-five years, selecting a representative sample, and ordering them into coherent themes. He has also written an introduction to the whole collection and to each section, providing the reader with a helpful summary of my thinking.

At first I was rather skeptical about the value of any such collection. My most coherent thinking can be found in the three internationally published books: *Jesus before Christianity, God in South Africa,* and *Jesus Today: A Spirituality of Radical Freedom.* But as I read through what Stan had put together and his perceptive introductions, I came to realize that these essays, articles, and talks might well be of considerable benefit to many more people than the small numbers to whom they were originally addressed.

The collection is, of course, diverse and uneven. There are a few academic articles, there are essays that formed parts of other collections, and there are talks that were subsequently printed as booklets as well as talks that have never appeared in print. There is also one sermon: a recent Good Friday sermon. Consequently, some of the chapters have footnotes while others do not. The original audiences varied from academics to priests and religious, from politicians to ecumenical gatherings. Moreover the circumstances varied from that of the apartheid era to our present postapartheid years.

There has been a large measure of consistency in my thinking over the years, although I do not think I would formulate some things today as I did twenty or more years ago. Each essay or talk has a definite historical context. The collection, however, has not been ordered chronologically, but rather groups essays and talks according to themes.

Since many readers, especially younger readers, will not be acquainted with the history of South Africa and the struggle against apartheid, I would like to add something about the concrete historical context in which these essays and my three books were written.

South Africa has sometimes been called a rainbow nation. While the majority of our people are of African descent, others are of European, Indian, and Indonesian ancestry, not to mention those whose ancestry is mixed. Immigrants have been pouring into the country from all over the world, including other African countries, for nearly four centuries. However, from the time of their arrival as settlers in 1652, the Europeans colonized and dominated everyone else. While a considerable amount of mixing took place at first, most people of European descent regarded themselves as superior and practiced some form of racial segregation and discrimination.

In 1948, the white government formalized this segregation by setting up an extremely unjust and oppressive social and political system known as apartheid. Only people of pure European ancestry would have the vote, meaning that the vast majority of the people were excluded. They had no say at all and no privileges.

It was an extremely complicated social and political system, but all that needs to be noted here is that it was a form of racial injustice and oppression that cried to heaven for vengeance. The churches were slow to appreciate this point. One of the excuses was that the church should not interfere in politics. A number of us felt that that approach was, to say the least, very bad theology. That exercise also gave me the reason for writing my first book: *Jesus before Christianity* (1976). I wanted to show, among other things, that Jesus did not exclude politics from his concerns and his preaching. In fact, in those days there was no separation between religion and politics because God cannot be excluded from any area of life.

I am a South African of European descent, but as a Christian and as a Dominican preacher I felt compelled to denounce in no uncertain terms the system of apartheid. The apartheid government had tried to justify the system theologically. That challenged me and numerous others to reject as heretical this kind of theology. Some of the essays in this collection are evidence of this theological struggle.

The reader will notice that one of the essays first appeared in a book in honor of Dr. Beyers Naudé and another in a book in honor of Archbishop Desmond Tutu. These two men were some of the great heroes of the church struggle against apartheid. Dr. Naudé was a former moderator of the all-white Dutch Reformed Church. His conversion was a powerful witness in South Africa. Archbishop Tutu was the head of the Anglican Church.

The highlight of this kind of condemnation of apartheid and criticism of the rather cautious statements of the church about apartheid was the famous Kairos Document. In 1985, some 153 of us signed that document, which was subtitled "A Challenge to the Churches." We came from a broad spectrum of churches, and we decided to name what we were calling for "a prophetic theology."

We were persecuted by the regime, as we called it, for our involvement in the Kairos Document. Some were arrested and detained. Others like myself went into hiding, and while I was in hiding I wrote my second book: *God in South Africa* (1988). This book was my attempt to write a comprehensive theological reflection upon apartheid and the struggle against apartheid in terms of sin and salvation—an example of contextual theology.

By this time, the apartheid regime had become, in desperation, even more oppressive and repressive. Imprisonment, torture, and killings were the order of the day. More and more people joined the struggle, including many Christians and members of other faiths. Eventually, by February 1990, the regime suddenly decided to begin the search for a negotiated settlement. Thus began three years of remarkable negotiations and compromises that led to our first democratic elections in April 1994.

The ANC (African National Congress) won the election with a large majority, and Nelson Mandela became our first democratic president. At first, everything seemed to be going well, and everybody was bending over backward to accommodate others. We call it our honeymoon period. The problems emerged gradually: crime, corruption, nepotism, inefficiency, greed, conflicts, power struggles, personality clashes, and rivalries—not unlike most other countries in the world. Our social and political context had changed. Many South Africans, like others around the globe, had entered a new age: an age of despair. Others, however, have remained hopeful despite the setbacks.

While we had achieved some measure of social and political liberation and while we still needed to struggle for economic liberation, what we needed right now, together with the rest of the world, was personal freedom, a radical spirituality—hence my latest book, *Jesus Today: A Spirituality of Radical Freedom* (2006). It was my attempt to show that the spirituality that Jesus had lived and taught was even more relevant today than ever before and that our social activism needed a personal and spiritual underpinning. My most recent public lecture (2008) has been about hope in an age of despair. It has been placed at the head of this collection and gives the book its title.

—Albert Nolan

Introduction

Many thousands of readers have come to know Albert Nolan through his three best-selling books: *Jesus before Christianity* (1976), *God in South Africa* (1988), and *Jesus Today: A Spirituality of Radical Freedom* (2006). Apart from these books, however, Nolan has written many articles and given numerous talks. This book seeks to make a selection of such articles and talks accessible to a wider audience.

Most of the chapters in this book were written during the time of apartheid in South Africa. Apartheid was a system of racial segregation and discrimination enforced by the white minority government in South Africa from 1948 to 1994. It was one of the most violent and repressive regimes in the world, bringing pain and suffering to countless people. Yet the time of apartheid was a period of mixed experiences of hope and despair. As Nolan would describe it, it was "a time of tears and sadness that [was] nevertheless fraught with hope and joyful anticipation" (Nolan 1986d, 139). In such a context, in his talks and writings, Nolan sought to unleash the message and power of Christian hope. I believe that that message of hope, that yearning for a better world, remains particularly relevant in our world today, just as relevant as it was during the struggle against apartheid in South Africa.

Theology has often been described as faith seeking understanding. In today's global context, with our mixed experiences of gloom and hope, perhaps theology should be perceived as hope seeking understanding. Theology should emerge as a response to our questions about hope: What can Christian hope mean to those who are in despair in a world marked by poverty, global warming, global economic downturn, war, terrorism, and the collapse of human rights? What should Christian hope mean for those who believe that another world is possible and who are involved in global and local campaigns against poverty and injustice? I believe that Nolan's reflections on hope, written during the time of apartheid, can offer insights that would enable us to formulate and answer our own questions about hope today.

In November 2008, the Dominican order honored Nolan with the distinguished title "Master in Sacred Theology," in recognition of his lifetime contributions to theology in South Africa and the world. In accepting this honor, Nolan offered a lecture, "Hope in an Age of Despair," which is included here. In his lecture he referred to four themes on Christian hope: God as the basis of our hope, common good as the object of our hope, the value of adopting an attitude of hopefulness, and the value of acting hopefully. These themes supply the framework for organizing this volume.

Many people have contributed to making this book a reality. I would like to thank the vicar general for the Dominicans in southern Africa, Mark James, for initiating this project together with Albert, and for entrusting me with the editorial task. I am also grateful to Marion Jordaan, who assisted in the proofreading of the first manuscript. Most of all, I would like to thank Albert Nolan for allowing us to publish his articles and for sharing his gifts with us. I was privileged to work with him and learn a lot from his spiritual insights and vision, as well as his enduring patience, during the editing of the book. As I interacted with Nolan and as I read his various articles, I realized that one of the unique gifts that Nolan has as a theologian and as a Dominican is his ability to combine depth and simplicity in communicating the gospel message. I hope the book enables readers to appreciate the depth and simplicity of the gospel: the gospel of love, faith, and hope.

—Stan Muyebe

PART 1

Background

Albert Nolan's lecture "Hope in an Age of Despair" offers an appropriate starting point, offering insights that find expression in most of the pieces in this book. The opening chapter is followed by two pieces that elucidate Nolan's work as a contextual theologian and as a member of the Dominican Order of Preachers. In fact, these two identities are closely linked.

The starting point for Nolan's theology is the experiences of the poor and the oppressed, especially their experiences of pain and suffering. In Nolan's writings, the poor and the oppressed are called "those sinned against" because they are victims of structural sin. For Nolan, the gospel that we preach fails to be good news if it is not first and foremost the good news for those sinned against. He wrote, "The Gospel that we preach will not be a Gospel of Jesus Christ unless it takes sides with those who are sinned against—the poor and the oppressed" (Nolan 1988, xii).

In his writings, as a theologian and as a Dominican, Nolan is therefore concerned with the following question: How do we release the gospel from its Western trappings and recover it as good news, as a message of hope, for those sinned against? To be able to achieve this objective, Nolan realizes that it is important to read and contemplate on the word of God in the Bible, not only from a priori principles drawn from Western theology, but also from the vantage point of those sinned against—specifically, those suffering and fighting against the system of apartheid. Their experiences of pain and suffering, as well as their categories of thought and expression, should inform the way a Dominican theologian reads and interprets the Bible. The contemplation on the word of God, and the subsequent preaching that is the fruit of this contemplation, should be done, not in an abstract way, but in relation to the experiences and questions of the poor and the oppressed. The Dominican contemplation and preaching that emerges should offer a message of hope to the poor, a message that is relevant and enriching to the poor and the oppressed. This imperative has colored and shaped the spirit and content of Nolan's theological work.

CHAPTER 1

Hope in an Age of Despair

The theology in which I and others have been engaged in South Africa has been described as contextual theology. The theological questions we dealt with were questions that arose out of our social context, which for the most part was the social context of apartheid and the struggle against apartheid. The context today is different—very different. It is far more complex and not so easy to analyze and define.

One great characteristic of our times, however—throughout the world and particularly in South Africa—is despair. We live in an age of despair. For centuries, we experienced hopefulness and optimism of one kind or another—political, economic, scientific, and religious. Now suddenly almost everyone has been plunged into a state of despair. This is our new context, or at least the most deeply felt mood of our times.

In this context we as Christians are called upon, in the words of the First Letter of Peter, "to give an account of the hope that is in us." We begin with a brief analysis of the hopefulness of the past that has now given way to the hopelessness of today.

Our Age of Despair

The seventeenth century in Europe gave birth to a great burst of optimism. It was called the Age of Reason. The philosophers

---

This is a slightly expanded version of a lecture that was delivered on November 15, 2008, on the occasion of Nolan receiving from the Dominican Order the title of STM (Master in Sacred Theology).

and scientists of the time broke away from the authoritarianism of the church, and, making use of reason alone, they became enthusiastically optimistic about what was called "human progress." They were convinced that by relying upon reason and scientific thinking, human beings would be able to solve all their problems. Gradually, step by step, this dream turned into a nightmare. There were many gains and benefits, but again and again human beings turned out to be unreasonable, cruel, and selfish. Today very few people would still believe that science, technology, and reason alone might solve all our problems.

The French Revolution and the Russian Revolution became violent and oppressive. Nazi Germany became thoroughly inhuman. Colonialism was anything but reasonable and progressive.

Then there was the hopeful age of capitalistic expansion and the free-market economy. The market would solve all our problems, provided that we didn't interfere with it or regulate it. The prospect of limitless economic growth and economic development throughout the world created an amazing amount of hopefulness. It lasted quite a long time. But now, that bubble has also burst as banks fall and economies falter because the market has failed us. For some people this is just one more reason to despair, especially since it means that the poor will get poorer even faster than before.

Earlier on, throughout the world, many millions had based their hope for the future on the development of a socialist world of equality and sharing. But as communist governments in Eastern Europe and the Soviet Union became more totalitarian and oppressive, and eventually collapsed, this hope was dashed to the ground, too.

In the church too, there is a growing feeling of despondency. The Second Vatican Council had filled many of us with hopeful excitement about the future of the church. It seemed as if we were beginning to move away from an authoritarian, hierarchical church to the radical freedom of Jesus and the gospel. But since then, almost all the gains of the Council have been, slowly but surely, undermined and reversed.

Add to this the sex scandals and the way they were covered up by the church, together with the present lack of vocations to the priesthood and religious life, and what you have is a formula for demoralization and despair.

In South Africa an enormous amount of hope was generated by the struggle itself and by its success in dismantling apartheid, by the negotiated settlement, by the relatively peaceful transition to democracy, by our new constitution, and by the charismatic leadership of Mandela. But since then our hopes have been gradually eroded, and today the general mood can only be described as disillusionment and despair. Of course there are exceptions. Some do remain hopeful.

However, not everyone is in a state of despair. There are some signs of hope, like the new pro-poor governments in Latin America and the election of Barack Obama in the United States. But on the whole, the signs we see point to yet greater doom and gloom, to yet more suffering and misery for the poor.

Looming over all of this like a dark, threatening cloud is the reality of global warming and climate change, and the lack of sufficient political will to make the necessary changes to save the planet. Those who work in this area of concern are beginning to doubt that human life will survive on this planet—let alone other forms of life.

Nevertheless, what I want to argue is that this shift from hope to hopelessness is not a disaster. It is a magnificent new opportunity for the development of genuine Christian hope.

Christian Hope

For a Christian there *is* hope. There is always hope. In the words of Paul, we hope against hope—that is to say, we remain hopeful even when there appear to be no signs of hope at all.

Why? Because our hope is not based upon signs. Our hope is based upon God and God alone. We put all our hope and trust in God. Or at least we try to do so.

But what does it mean to put all one's hope and trust in God? That, I suggest, is the major theological question of our time. It is a particularly difficult question, because for very many people today God is dead or irrelevant, a meaningless concept. To many, putting all one's hope and trust in God sounds like a pious cop-out.

What does it mean, then, to trust God?

In the first place, to quote from Psalm 146, it means that we do not put our trust in princes.

> Do not put your trust in princes,
> in mortals in whom there is no help. . . .
> Happy are those . . .
> whose hope is in the Lord their God. (146:3, 5)

We cannot rely upon the promises of princes: political princes or industrial princes or even princes of the church.

Having good leaders is obviously helpful, but ultimately we cannot base our hope for the future upon human leaders of any kind—not only because all humans including ourselves are fallible, weak, and liable to make mistakes, but more important because none of us, individually or together, is powerful or all-knowing enough to save the world.

Nor can we put all our hope and confidence in human institutions of any kind: political parties, churches, governments, or electricity suppliers. They can all flounder and fail.

Nor can we base our hope for the future upon any kind of ideology: the ideologies of socialism or the free market or even democracy.

To put all one's hope and trust in God means that, while we might value and appreciate the contribution of princes and institutions and ideologies, in the end we simply do not treat them as the absolute and unshakeable basis of our hopes for the future. Just how unreliable all these things are is precisely what we are beginning to discover today.

The final temptation is to trust nobody but ourselves. "I seem to be the only one who knows what is best for the world. If only they would all just listen to me."

On the other hand if we don't trust anyone or anything, not even our own ideas, life becomes completely impossible. I have to put some measure of trust in the pilot who flies the plane or the scientists who prepared the medicine I take or the doctor who diagnoses my illness. They are not infallible, and I take a calculated risk when I trust them. But in the final analysis I cannot put all my hope and trust in any of them, nor even in myself.

Of course, there are people whose trust in God is unhealthy too. It can become a cop-out, a way of escaping the need to act wisely and vigorously. Much depends on how we see God. But much also depends upon what we are hoping for. We live in an age of despair, not only because people had built their hopes upon shaky foundations, but also because many of us had been hoping for all the wrong things.

What Do We Hope For?

The object of Christian hope is the coming of God's kingdom, God's reign on earth. In the Our Father we pray, "Thy kingdom come; thy will be done on earth." Our hope is that God's will be done on earth.

Many people today find the idea of God's will difficult to appreciate. Others are all too ready to think they know exactly what God wants and what God's kingdom will be like.

We can be sure of one thing, however: that God's will is not arbitrary. When we speak about "my" will, we are often referring to something arbitrary, my arbitrary choice about what ought to be done. To impose that upon others would be decidedly oppressive.

God's will is different. What God wills is always the common good. What God wants is whatever is best for all of us together, whatever is best for the whole of creation.

Of course it is not always easy for us to appreciate what is best for everyone. But if our attempts are to do, as far as possible, whatever is for the common good, then we are doing God's will, and to that extent God's will is being done on earth.

Some people will assume that what is best for everyone will not be best for me as an individual, and that what is best for me will clash with the needs of others and the common good. That is not true. What is best for everyone is also best for me. In other words, God's will is a way of saying that what is best for everyone is best for me, too—even if I find it very difficult to do.

The object of Christian hope then is the common good.

The problem with the hopefulness of the past is that it was too often a hope for something that would not have served the common good of all human beings and all of creation. The object of these hopes has been too often selfish and self-serving, egocentric and narrow-minded: hopes for a better future for myself, my family, and my own country at the expense of other people; hopes for economic growth and a higher standard of living for some, regardless of others. That is not God's will or the common good.

Trusting God's Work

When we work for the common good (and many people are doing that all over the world), our work becomes a participation in God's work. We have seen that, as Christians, the basis of our hope is God and the object of our hope is God's will. But perhaps it would be more helpful to say that what we rely upon is God's work.

God is at work in the whole universe and always has been. God is the one who has brought everything into existence and keeps everything moving forward in the immense unfolding of the universe.

God has been at work in all of human history and continues to be involved in the world of politics, economics, and religion—not to mention what we call nature. Last but not least, God is at work in you and me. There is no area of life from which God can be excluded.

That does not mean that everything is good and that we are not responsible for what happens in our lives. Obviously much is wrong, and we might even say evil. But God remains involved in ways that are supremely mysterious.

Ultimately the cause of all that is wrong or sinful or evil is human selfishness. We cannot go into that now, but we can take heart from the belief that God is at work nevertheless and in a way all that will change, eventually, when God's will is done on earth as it is in heaven.

God's work cannot fail. It is totally reliable.

Christian hope then, the hope that Jesus taught us, means relying completely on God's work in all things—that is to say, it means relying upon the goodness of the great unfolding of the universe of which we are a part.

Where Is Your God?

In the final analysis then, everything depends upon our belief in God and God's great work. Hope is based upon faith—belief in God. If our faith is weak, our hope will be shaky, too. As Jesus said again and again, "Your faith has saved you."

The problem today is that it is not easy to believe in God, or rather to understand what belief in God might mean. However, some things about God are becoming clearer. For example, with regard to the great problem of suffering in the world, we have moved from seeing God as the *cause* of this suffering, to seeing God as the one who *allows* people to suffer, to seeing God as the one *who is suffering* with us. God is to be found among the victims of injustice, those who are sinned against, the poor and the marginalized, the sick and the outcasts.

That is what Jesus taught us. That is the meaning of the crucifixion. Jesus was a victim of human cruelty.

But what is the use of a powerless, suffering God? How can we put all our hope and trust in such a God? We can and we must, because God is powerful—all-powerful—not with the power of force or coercion, but with the power of compassion and love. The oppressive power of brute force and violence can never be the basis of Christian hope. It is not God's power, not God's way of acting.

As I said earlier, we hope against hope. We continue to hope even when there are no visible signs of hope. We recognize the darkness and apparent hopelessness of the present situation and put all our trust in God. Then, gradually, as our eyes adjust to the darkness of despair, we begin to see the emerging shapes or outlines of God's great and mysterious work—the finger of God, as Jesus called it. These are the paradoxical signs of the time that only become visible once we believe that God is at work in our world, once we learn to look at life with an attitude of hopefulness.

We have time for only a few random examples.

A leading peace activist says that the much-publicized war in Iraq has led to an exponential increase in the number of people actively involved in the peace movement worldwide. Is this the finger of God drawing good out of evil?

The terrible suffering of so many people in violent conflicts, earthquakes, tsunamis, and pandemics like HIV/AIDS may give rise to despair in some, but it also elicits huge waves of compassion. What the world needs more than anything else is more compassion. Is this the enigmatic work of God?

The recent collapse of so many banks and corporations has been universally attributed to the greed of the super-rich. Up until now, the super-rich were heroes. They had made it to the top. But now it is not only the poor who see them as the culprits, the criminals whose greed we all have to pay for. Is that kind of discovery the work of God's mysterious providence?

The reaction of so many Catholics to the sex abuse scandals, their concern about the victims and about the callousness of some church leaders, has contributed powerfully to a new awareness of how much the church needs to change. Was this perhaps a happy fault, a blessing in disguise?

And would Barack Obama's call for change have received such a tremendous response in America and elsewhere if it had not been preceded by the neoconservative stupidity of George Bush and his advisors.

But most of all, I wonder if the present age of despair is not being used by God to challenge us to take God more seriously as the only basis for hope in the world. Is God writing straight again with crooked lines, as St. Augustine used to say?

And is that not what the death and resurrection of Jesus is about? Jesus' death, and especially his shameful death by crucifixion, plunged his disciples and many others into a state of despair. On the road to Emmaus the two disciples said, "We had hoped that he was the one to redeem Israel." But his rejection by the leaders and the chief priests and the people dashed all those hopes to the ground. On the cross Jesus himself felt abandoned by God: "My God, my God, why have you forsaken me?"

But those who continued to trust God, in spite of all this, as Jesus himself had done, gradually came to see the finger of God at work in this terrible tragedy. They began to see that Jesus was alive and active in a surprisingly new way. That he had risen from the dead and that his Spirit was now in them. That the cross was not a total failure. That it was paradoxically the triumph of God's work in the world. That it was our salvation and our hope for the future.

Here again we have God writing straight with crooked lines.

And that is why for Christians the resurrection is the great symbol of our hope. It is not the basis of our hope. The basis of our hope is God, and God alone. The resurrection is the finger of God we can see at work when we put all our hope and trust in God, when we begin to see dimly in the dark that Jesus is still at work in our world.

What matters in the long run, though, is not only that we are hopeful but that we act hopefully. The most valuable contribution that a Christian can make in our age of despair is to continue, because of our faith, to act hopefully, and in that way to be an encouragement to those who have lost all hope.

CHAPTER 2

The Art of Teaching Theology

"Ask, and it will be given you;
search, and you will find;
knock, and the door will be opened for you.
For everyone who asks receives,
and everyone who searches finds,
and for everyone who knocks, the door will be opened."
(Matt. 7:7–8; Luke 11:9–10 [NRSV])

Many centuries ago Anselm defined theology as *fides quaerens intellectum,* faith seeking understanding. To seek understanding is to ask questions and search for answers. It is not without reason that many of the great theological texts, like the *Summa* of Thomas Aquinas, have been set out as a series of questions and answers. Theology is by definition an attempt to answer faith questions.

What we have to notice, though, is that different people in different times and places ask different questions about their faith. What was a burning question in the early church or in the Middle Ages may turn out to be a question of no consequence to anyone today. We no longer fight on the streets about the number of persons or natures in Jesus Christ as they did in earlier times. And if I raised the medieval question of

---

This was originally published in Gabrielle Kelly and Kevin Saunders, eds., *Toward the Intelligent Use of Liberty: Dominican Approaches in Education* (Adelaide, Australia: ATP Press, 2007).

transubstantiation today, very few people would know what I was talking about. In our very different circumstances of life we grapple with different questions. Nor are these questions the same, even today, in different parts of the world or for different social groups in the same part of the world.

Different questions give rise to different theologies. There is one faith, but there are many theologies. Christian faith, as a commitment to God in Jesus Christ, remains the same at all times and in all circumstances. But theology, as the attempt to answer questions about this faith, will vary according to the different historical and social contexts that give rise to different questions.

Of course, we also have the phenomenon of different answers to the same questions, and in the past we tended to see the difference between the various schools of theology as simply a matter of different answers to the same questions. What was often not noticed was that there were some people who were asking totally different questions.

Our faith questions, then, are always contextual, one of the results of which is that our answers are contextual, too. That is not to say that our different theologies are totally relative and arbitrary. Any sound theology has to find its answers in the Bible and in Jesus himself as the incarnate Word of God. But my context, my assumptions, and my questions provide me with a particular perspective on the Bible and on the meaning of Jesus' life and death. This perspective can either open my eyes to what is already there in the Bible or it can blind me to what Jesus was actually saying.

When the poor, for example, read the Bible with serious questions about God's will for them, they discover that the Bible has much to say about poverty and oppression. On the other hand, those who live in another social context with no firsthand experience of poverty and oppression often overlook what is being said about these matters in the Bible. Whole theologies have been constructed without any reference to social justice because those people who constructed such theologies lived in a social context where questions about poverty and oppression did not arise at all, let alone as faith questions.

The Awareness of Contextuality

Only gradually did we began to discover the profound and all-embracing influence of contextuality upon all theology. I can remember my own discovery as a young Dominican that the theology of Thomas Aquinas was thoroughly time-bound and contextual. That did not lead me to reject Thomism. It was an exciting discovery that enabled me to appreciate Thomas all the more. He was a truly original theologian because he tackled the new questions of his age, questions that others had preferred to ignore. The pagan philosophy of Aristotle and the Muslim commentaries on the works of Aristotle had recently been introduced into the universities. That gave rise to a whole new set of questions and problems. Thomas tackled these questions boldly and answered them brilliantly.

But it is not only the *philosophical* assumptions of a particular period that give rise to new faith questions. The political and economic assumptions of that time or place might also give rise to new questions. Sometimes current political events can also present a challenge to our understanding of our faith. A good example of this would be Augustine's theology of the City of God. The political event was the fall of the Roman Empire. Augustine developed an elaborate theology in answer to the question, how can a Christian make sense of the fall of the Roman Empire?

Christianity and the Roman Empire had been closely associated with one another in the minds of most educated Christians. It took a brilliant thinker like Augustine to find a way of making sense of the empire's fall and helping his contemporaries to be hopeful about the future of Christianity. Augustine's famous distinction between the City of God and the City of Man [*sic*] was his answer to a very contextual question.

But even before we discovered the contextual character

of our traditional theologies, we had begun to recognize the contextuality of the Bible itself. Biblical criticism had made us aware of the *Sitz im Leben* or life contexts of various biblical texts. These contexts were not only historical, liturgical, cultural, and philosophical but also political and economic. All of this has revolutionized the study of the Bible.

Awareness of the contextuality of all theological formulations does not minimize their value, but it does present the teacher of theology with a pedagogical challenge. In all cases we need to explain the context that gave rise to the question that is being answered in this theological formulation. In the days when I tried to teach the theology of Thomas Aquinas to Dominican students, I found that I would have to spend most of the time in class explaining the question, so that the students could appreciate the brilliance of Thomas's answer. To appreciate the questions, one had to be, among other things, thoroughly conversant with Greek philosophy. That is why the seminary course had to begin with years of study in Greek philosophy.

I can remember the day I stopped in my tracks with the thought: *Why do I have to teach these people answers to questions they never ask? What about the very serious faith questions that they do have, but are not given an opportunity to ask?*

Eventually I came to the conclusion that the real value of studying the great theologians of the past was to learn how to go about answering our own faith questions and the questions of our contemporaries. What we learn from Thomas is how to be fearless in raising new questions and thorough in searching for answers.

Contextual Theologies Today

Most of the theologies that have developed in recent times have been consciously contextual. I am thinking of theologies like feminist theology, black theology, African theology, Asian theology, Latin American liberation theology, and so forth. All theologies are contextual, but not all theologians are fully aware of the contextuality of their questions and their answers. These new theologies are different because they are explicitly and intentionally contextual.

Feminist theology, for example, is a conscious attempt to do theology from within the experience of being a woman in a patriarchal world. This theology deals explicitly with the faith questions of women, and answers are developed from the perspective, experience, and insights of women. Most other theologies down through the ages have been constructed by men. They were answering the questions that men ask. The context was thoroughly patriarchal and oppressive, but male theologians were either totally blind to this or they thought that it made no difference to their theology. They saw their questions and their answers as valid for everybody. Male theologians would not have dreamed of calling their theology masculine theology or patriarchal theology. They were unaware of the contextuality of what they were doing theologically.

In a similar way, black theology is a conscious attempt to do theology from within the experience of black oppression. Since most white Christians are racist, black Christians begin to ask questions about the meaning of their faith. Is God white? Does God favor whites? Or is God on the side of oppressed black people?

Much of the theology we inherit is, in fact, white theology, but it is generally not conscious of its racial bias. White theology sees itself as a universal theology applicable to all peoples.

African theology is not the same as black theology. The context for black theology is the experience of being oppressed because you are black. The context for African theology is culture, African culture. The questions that are being dealt with in this theology are the questions that arise for people who are steeped in the cultures of Africa, cultures that are often very different from Western culture. In Africa people want to know whether their Christian faith is compatible with the veneration of ancestors and with traditional healing methods, the divining of spirits, and so forth.

Western theology grapples with the questions raised by Western culture and especially the modern questions of secularization. But these are treated as universal questions, and Western theology is thought of as equally applicable to all people of all cultures. Until recently, Western theology was unaware of its own contextuality.

Asian theology has a similar problem with the theological imperialism of the West. Asians have different faith questions because they are part of a very different culture or cultures.

Liberation theology is a largely Latin American attempt to answer the questions raised by the poor and their sympathizers who wanted to join the struggle for political liberation in their countries. It raised questions about the capitalistic assumptions of much of Western theology and tried to discern what God wished to say to the poor and the oppressed.

Kairos theology was the name given to a thoroughly contextual South African theology that was a response to the crisis (*kairos*) created by the apartheid regime when it declared that all Christians were obliged to obey the government because of what Paul says in Romans 13:1–7. This theology arose at the height of apartheid when the regime was tear-gassing, imprisoning, and killing protesting schoolchildren. Questions about the meaning of Christian faith in these circumstances were being asked, and the people were clamoring for answers.

Professional theologians were consulted, but in the end the Christian people themselves, those who had no particular credentials or authority, wrote the now famous 1985 Kairos Document. They condemned the theology of the government in no uncertain terms, challenged the churches to speak out no matter what the consequences might be, and proposed a prophetic theology of action against the tyranny of apartheid.

These and other consciously contextual theologies have given rise to a query about who can do theology.

Who Can Do Theology?

Almost all the theologies we have inherited and often still teach in our seminaries and universities were developed and continue to be developed in an academic context. In other words, the questions that most professional theologians have been grappling with have been questions that arise out of what other professional theologians have said. For centuries, academic theologians, both Catholic and Protestant, have been engaged in arguments with one another in their own abstract and technical jargon that very few outside of their circles have been able to understand.

Until recently, this academic theology was constrained even further by being exclusively male, predominantly clerical, and, in the case of Catholics, largely celibate. The very real faith questions of the poor, of the uneducated, of women, of the laity, of black people, and of married people were not regarded as relevant to the construction of a theology. And whenever these questions were taken into account, they were filtered through the narrow minds of white, male, and clerical academics.

All of this is changing now and changing fast. The tendency is for theology to move out onto the streets to face new questions arising out of nonacademic contexts. This change raises questions about who does theology. This is not simply a matter of including blacks, women, and laity among professional theologians. If theology is faith seeking understanding, then anyone with faith can do theology because anyone with faith can seek to understand their faith by asking questions and seeking answers. Nor should we assume that the average believer does not know how to ask questions or that they are incapable of finding answers.

In many parts of the church today, Catholics are not encouraged to ask questions about the meaning of their faith. Sometimes we are even given the impression that if we ask questions it must be because our faith is weak. We are told that we have become doubting Thomases or that, like Peter walking on the water, we are men and women of little faith. This is simply not true.

We ask questions in order to strengthen our faith, not weaken it. We ask questions in order to understand our faith better and to see how it relates to the circumstances in which we live. And if we do have doubts, it is better to air them than to hide and suppress them. Questions and doubts can spur us on to search and to keep searching until we find answers, to knock and keep knocking until the door is opened.

In some Catholic circles it is very difficult to get people to ask real searching questions. In teaching theology I have often found that it takes many hours and even days of explanation before some Catholics will take the risk of expressing a doubt or asking a serious question. However, once they feel sufficiently free to do so, the questions pour out like an unstoppable flood.

Encouraging students to ask questions is a good pedagogical method in the teaching of any subject. But in theology it has an added meaning because the foundation upon which you are building as a teacher is the faith of the students. Their questions should be faith questions.

Part of the art of teaching theology is the skill of helping one's students to avoid asking questions for the sake of asking questions or out of mere curiosity, but to raise the issues that really affect their faith and their Christian practice. Theology is faith seeking understanding. In other words, my questions arise out of my commitment in faith to Jesus Christ. You cannot do theology without faith.

Finding Answers

Many people are looking for instant answers: sound bites. When you have opened the floodgates and the questions come pouring in, the temptation is to offer quick and easy answers.

Whether the theology teacher or someone else in the group provides such answers, they are seldom helpful. To do theology well, one needs to be able to hold the question, park it if need be, and even spend time analyzing the question itself. Why do we ask that question? Nor should we be satisfied with the first answer that comes to mind. One's intuitive and spontaneous answer is valuable, but what do others think? Answering questions of faith should be a community exercise. We all need to listen to what those who share our faith have to say. We need to listen to one another, to well-informed theologians, and to those who have authority in the church (the magisterium). Above all, we need to listen to Jesus himself, whom we believe to be the Word or revelation of God.

Listening to all these voices may not provide us with a clear and consistent answer. The search must then continue. "Search and you will find," Jesus says. "Knock and the door will be opened." What we are dealing with, in the final analysis, is not a mere academic subject, but the faith of the people we are trying to teach. Just as the questions they ask must be faith questions, so also the answers they should be looking for would have to be faith answers. In other words, in one very important sense the answers will come from the faith commitment of the student. In that sense the answers will be the work of the Holy Spirit.

The art of teaching theology is, among other things, the art of allowing the Spirit to work in the student and in the classroom as a whole. In that way, the students learn to do their own theology and come to a deeper understanding of their faith.

CHAPTER 3

Preaching and Contemplation

Contemplative preaching is by no means a new phenomenon. It has been the way of preaching of the prophets, the saints, and the mystics through the ages. And even today it is the way of preaching of all really good and authentic preachers. They would not call it "contemplative" preaching. That is my word. In fact, many truly holy and effective preachers may not even refer to their prayer life as contemplative.

While we will, of necessity, be referring frequently to the preacher as the one who stands up before an audience in a church, contemplative preaching can happen in any number of other ways.

The teacher in the classroom and the professor in the lecture hall can give to their listeners the fruits of their contemplation. The author and the journalist can do the same. Discussion and dialogue in workshops and seminars could be places where the results of contemplative prayer are experienced.

A specially privileged place for this kind of communication, though, is the counseling session. *Contemplata aliis tradere* can happen very powerfully within the context of counseling or spiritual direction. But it can also happen in less obvious ways, like parents giving advice to their children, friends sharing their

---

This is a slightly abbreviated version of a chapter in a book dedicated to Damian Byrne, master of the Dominican Order, who reminded us of our vocation as preachers (Michael Monshau, ed., *The Grace and Task of Preaching* [Dublin: Dominican Publications, 2006]).

insights, leaders giving public addresses, and meetings in the workplace. To contemplate and to give to others the fruits of our contemplation is something that we are all challenged to do wherever and whenever we can—in season and out of season. Francis of Assisi is said to have told his friars to preach at all times and when necessary to use words.

We have all suffered under bad preachers in our churches, not only those who talk nonsense, those who never prepare and who preach more or less the same sermon every Sunday, but also those who just criticize, condemn, and lay down the law. On the other hand, there are a growing number of preachers whose sermons are informative and interesting, especially in their interpretation of Scripture and the teaching of the church.

Contemplative preaching, however, does something more than this, something different. It is not merely a matter of *doctrina aliis tradere*, giving to others the teaching of the church, its doctrines and dogmas. Nor is it a matter of *theologia aliis tradere*, handing on to others the latest theology or scriptural exegesis. *Contemplata aliis tradere* means communicating to others what we ourselves have learned from our own experience of faith and contemplation.

We live in a postmodern world. On the whole, people are no longer looking for doctrines and dogmas or grand systems of theology. The Age of the Enlightenment with its total reliance upon logic and rationality is over. Most people no longer believe that human beings will eventually overcome the world's problems and that progress is inevitable. That was modernity. What people believe in today is not reason and universal theories, but experience.

The world as we experience it is profoundly irrational. Things do not always make sense, and if we are going to be honest we must admit that often enough we have no explanation for the things we experience, like massacres, torture, the sexual abuse of small children, and the maiming of innocent people—to name but a few. Even the grand certainties of science are now being discovered to be mistaken. In quantum physics and astronomy as well as sciences like biology, scientists are coming face to face with the limits of human knowledge—with the mystery of it all.

Of course, there are those who cannot cope with all this uncertainty and insecurity. They are the ones who seek a haven in fundamentalism of one kind or another—religious fundamentalism, scientific fundamentalism, or even economic fundamentalism. They cling desperately to their absolute truths no matter what happens. They rely blindly on those they regard as authorities.

By and large, though, people today are suspicious of ideologies, dogmas, doctrines, and any other absolute truths. They are looking for authenticity rather than authority. They want to hear an honest and sincere witness rather than a certified authority. Recent scandals in the church have only reinforced this reluctance to put one's trust in the words of those who exercise authority.

Besides, with such a plurality of voices and authorities competing with one another and even killing one another, the postmodern attitude has become one of tolerance. People have learned to live with fragmentation and plurality. Difference and otherness are treated as interesting and informative rather than as a problem.

Postmodernism is not the latest philosophy of a few highly educated and disillusioned thinkers in the North. It is a general attitude of mind that is growing fast in the North and the South, and especially among the youth whatever their cultural heritage might be. The only exceptions would be fundamentalists, the older generation, isolated rural communities, and those who are so poor that survival is their sole preoccupation.

The postmodern attitude of mind is not necessarily an obstacle to the preaching of the good news of Jesus Christ. In fact, it could be seen as an unprecedented opportunity. It often leads to a greater interest than before in our Christian experience of spirituality, meditation, contemplation, prayer, mysticism, and inner peace.

However, if the good news is presented as *doctrina* or *theologia*, it will not be heard. Not because the *contemplata*, the things that have emerged from our contemplation, are totally different from *doctrina* and *theologia*, but because the message comes across quite differently when the preacher is not just a parrot repeating the doctrines and laws of the church or the latest theology found in books, but a man or woman of prayer who has internalized the word of God and speaks from experience and with obvious sincerity.

But it is more than that. A life that is seriously committed to contemplation will produce fruits that will transform the whole experience of preaching—for the preacher and the listener. We will explore something of what this might mean for preaching after a brief look at contemplation today and especially the Dominican tradition of contemplation.

Contemplation Today

While originally contemplation was thought of as the calling of all Christians, for a long time now Catholics have regarded it as the special vocation of a chosen few: monks, nuns, and hermits. The rest of us are said to be engaged in the active life. Somewhere along the way the whole tradition of contemplative prayer was lost or at least badly neglected—even by monks and nuns. Today there is a very powerful movement throughout Christianity of returning to the Catholic tradition of contemplation and meditation. Even more important, this widespread movement includes the revival of the original tradition that contemplation is for everyone and not only for the privileged few. A growing number of laypeople, as well as religious and clergy, meditate, practice centering prayer, and give themselves to contemplation and mysticism.

This new movement has been deepened and developed by

the discoveries of the new cosmology and by the emerging spirituality of the ecological movement. Contemplating the grandeur of God in the marvels of an expanding and evolving universe, of which we are such a tiny part, adds a new dimension to the experience of wonder and awe. . . .

Contemplation is described almost universally today as a form of consciousness or awareness. It is not so much a matter of changing reality as becoming aware of what is already there. Contemplation is the experience of waking up to reality, developing a heightened awareness of what is happening around us and within us, and above all having a deeper consciousness of the presence of God in everything.

Most people are hardly conscious at all. They are half asleep or living in a world of lies and illusions. Contemplation is a conscious attempt to dispel all the illusions we have about ourselves, about others, and about the world. It is a search for the truth about ourselves, about others, and about the universe we are part of, which is at the same time a search for God. Bernard McGinn, the renowned scholar of Christian spirituality and mysticism, defines mysticism as "the transformation of consciousness through a direct encounter with God."

Consciousness is something more than conceptual knowledge. Being conscious of God's presence is different from the intellectual assertion that God is everywhere. Nor is it simply a matter of feeling. We have learned to become conscious of our feelings and to learn from them, but contemplation is more than that. It is sometimes described as "unknowing" or recognizing that we don't know. God is the great unknown. In the end we have to throw out all we thought we knew about God to make contact with the great mystery, not through our thoughts or feelings but through an experience of wordless wonder and awe.

This is not the place to elaborate on these matters. Our concern is with the impact a life dedicated to contemplation would have on our preaching today.

The Fruits of Our Contemplation

When we say that we preach our *contemplata*, the fruits of our contemplation, we are referring not only to the verbal content of our preaching but also to the message we communicate by who we are and what we are, by our attitudes, and even by our body language. The fruits of contemplation include qualities like inner peace, freedom and fearlessness, a love for people, genuine humility, a spirit of hopefulness, gratitude and joy, and a profound sense of mystery. These fruits of our contemplative prayer characterize and shape what I call contemplative preaching.

The following list does not pretend to be comprehensive, but let's take a closer look at these qualities.

Inner Peace

What people today are thirsting for, whether they are postmodernists or fundamentalists, is inner peace. Among those who hear our preaching are deeply troubled souls who long for a message that will bring them peace, a peace the world cannot give. Such people will be quick to recognize that the preacher is a man or woman of deep inner peace—or not.

Inner peace is, among other things, the fruit of years of silent meditation. With all the stresses and strains of life today, our heads and hearts come to be cluttered with thoughts, plans, fears, resentments, desires, and conflicts. The practice of silent meditation or centering prayer helps us to calm the storms within us.

However, something more than that is needed. The contemplative is someone who has spent a lot of time trying to get to know himself or herself better. As we gradually come to face the truth about ourselves, we discover, among other things, that we are not free. We are chained like slaves to our comforts, our moods, our fears, our reputation, our achievements and successes, our health, our looks, our favorite devotions, our culture, our theological tradition, and our names for God. These are our attachments, our chains. We say we need them and cannot do without them. They are not necessarily bad, and we don't necessarily have to give them up. But we do need to become detached from them if we are ever to have inner peace.

Detachment, according to Eckhart, is more important than love, because without detachment we do not have the inner freedom to love others.[1] John of the Cross calls it purgation and takes us through the long painful process of "dark nights" on the way to freedom. Our paths may differ, but only after years of struggle in prayer can the contemplative enjoy the fruits of detachment and freedom.

It is this inner freedom that makes the contemplative preacher so fearless. No longer afraid of what people might think or say, the contemplative preacher is free to speak the truth regardless of the consequences.

Fearlessness and inner freedom are qualities we associate with prophets—those in every age who are bold enough to speak out when everyone else remains silent. For that reason, contemplative preaching becomes prophetic whenever the circumstances require.

Our freedom, fearlessness, and inner peace, to the extent that we have them, will shine through in our preaching. They will speak louder than our words, just as they did so magnificently in the preaching of Dominic, who was once described as "stupifyingly free." Was this not also one of the qualities that attracted people so powerfully to Jesus? He had no hang-ups, obsessions, or compulsions. He was free and fearless, and so obviously at peace with himself and with God.

A postmodern audience would appreciate nothing more than a preacher who shows himself or herself to be free and

---

[1]*Meister Eckhart: The Essential Sermons, Commentaries, Treatises, and Defense* (New York: Paulist Press, 1981), 285ff.

fearless—even when the postmodern listeners are not really free and fearless themselves.

A Love for People

The famous English Dominican Vincent McNabb is reputed to have said, "If you don't love [people], don't preach to them. Preach to yourself."

Genuine contemplative prayer helps us to overcome our selfishness and self-centeredness by making us more and more conscious of the unity of all things in God. Our separate individualized egos are illusions. The truth is that we all belong together; we are part of one another and part of the wonderful expanding universe that God is busy creating.

This kind of contemplative consciousness influences our preaching. We have from the start a deep sympathy and appreciation for the people to whom we are preaching. We feel with them in their struggles and their pain. We are able to forgive them in our hearts while we long to help them change whatever may need to be changed.

In other words, we don't begin by hating them. We don't hammer them and threaten them. We don't just condemn them and criticize them. We don't stand up there like self-righteous Pharisees who thank God that we are not like these sinful people. We love them and forgive them as Jesus did.

When our love for them is genuine and spontaneous, our postmodern listeners will recognize it and appreciate it. We are not playing games with them or venting our pent-up feelings on them. We are not trying to show them how learned we are and how well we can preach. We are not looking for praise and congratulations. We are not on some kind of ego trip. We care for them as we care for our very selves.

From this position of loving care the preacher is able to present, effectively and powerfully, the challenges of the gospel. No matter how demanding and difficult these challenges might appear to be, they will be heard and taken seriously.

Like Dominic, Catherine, and Eckhart, among others, our contemplative prayer will enable us to do this.

A *Spirit of Hopefulness*

In a way, all our preaching should be a matter of giving an account of the hope that is in us (1 Pet. 3:15). When we have no hope in us, when we have forgotten how to trust God, and when the chaos of today's world has led us to despair and cynicism, then that is what will come through in our preaching even as we talk about the good news and the hope of resurrection.

Pretending that we are hopeful when we are not is no good. All we can do in that case is preach from the heart about the struggle we are experiencing with our feelings of hopelessness. Our listeners will appreciate that kind of honesty, especially if we then encourage them and ourselves to go back to our search for God in prayer.

Hopefulness, as an attitude that imbues all we say and do, is one of the fruits of contemplation. Among other things it is the result of a life that is steeped in gratitude and thankfulness to God. In prayer we learn to thank God for the many, many good things in life, for nature, for the universe, for other people, for the wonder of human consciousness, and for each new day. Eventually this positive attitude of gratefulness begins to transform our consciousness, and gradually we come to shed our habitual negativity and pessimism.

Ronald Rolheiser sums up what many before him have said about gratitude: "To be a saint is to be motivated by gratitude, nothing more and nothing less."[2] In another place, he sums up Gutiérrez with the words, "Only one kind of person transforms the world spiritually, someone with a grateful heart."[3]

---

[2]*The Shattered Lantern: Rediscovering a Felt Knowledge of God*, rev. ed. (New York: Crossroad, 2001), 180.

[3]*The Holy Longing: The Search for a Christian Spirituality* (New York: Doubleday, 1999), 67.

While all contemplatives experience times of painful dryness and darkness, in the end one of the outstanding fruits of our faithfulness to contemplative prayer will be joy. So many preachers are not only dull and boring but so obviously joyless. How can we stand up there and preach the good news without rejoicing in one way or another?

We cannot compensate for our joylessness by telling jokes or poking fun at people we don't like. True joy comes from a deep sense of the presence of God in all things. The people were able to recognize that joy in Jesus, and they will be able to see at least something of it in the contemplative preacher today. Dominic was well known for his cheerfulness and joy.

The contemplative preacher is someone who comes across as a person who is full of hope, gratitude, and joy.

A Sense of Mystery

All contemplatives have a deep sense of mystery—the mystery of God, the mystery of life, the mysteries of our faith. Contemplation leads to a recognition of the serious limitations of all human knowledge. Eventually we discover that we don't know God, and what we thought we knew is, in fact, far off the mark. God becomes totally mysterious, and we go through a process that has been called "unknowing." Ironically that brings us much closer to God. But we now experience the presence of God in a cloud or in the dark—in mystery. Gradually we also begin to discover how mysterious we ourselves are and how mysterious all of God's creation is—not to speak of Jesus and what we call the mysteries of our faith. All is mystery, but that does not mean that all is lost. It means that everything is a marvel before which we can only stand in awe and wonder. Wonder is possibly the most profound form of consciousness.

The preaching of the contemplative is imbued with this powerful sense of mystery and wonder. How different our sermons would be if they presented life as a mystery to be enjoyed rather than as nothing more than a series of problems to be solved.

But more important, living in the presence of the truly awesome mystery whom we call God enables us to speak about God more authentically and from the heart. There are preachers today who avoid talking about God. They no longer know how to speak about God, and when they do so, God is clearly nothing more to them than an abstract idea. What a difference when the preacher is speaking about his or her own experience of a mystery they have contemplated in wonder and awe for many years.

These are high ideals, but they are also gifts from God that will be given to us in some measure if we are seriously committed to a life of contemplative prayer.

Preaching and teaching, when they flow from an abundance of contemplation, would be powerful and effective at any time and in any place. In our postmodern world especially, today and tomorrow, only some kind of contemplative preaching will capture the minds and hearts of our listeners.

Bibliography

Berry, Thomas. *The Dream of the Earth*. San Francisco: Sierra Club Books, 1988.

Colledge, E., and B. McGinn, eds. *Meister Eckhart: The Essential Sermons, Commentaries, Treatises, and Defense*. New York: Paulist Press, 1981.

Kaufman, Gordon D. *In Face of Mystery: A Constructive Theology*. Cambridge, Mass.: Harvard University Press, 1993.

Keating, Thomas. *Open Mind, Open Heart: The Contemplative Dimension of the Gospel*. New York: Continuum, 1995.

McGinn, Bernard. *The Mystical Thought of Meister Eckhart: The Man from Whom God Hid Nothing*. New York: Crossroad, 2001.

Rolheiser, Ronald. *The Holy Longing: The Search for a Christian Spirituality*. New York: Doubleday, 1999.

————. *The Shattered Lantern: Rediscovering a Felt Presence of God.* Rev. ed. New York: Crossroad, 2001.

Ruane, Edward M. "The Spirituality of the Preacher." In *In the Company of Preachers.* Aquinas Institute of Theology Faculty. Collegeville, Minn.: Liturgical Press, 1993.

Sheldrake, Philip. *Spirituality and Theology: Christian Living and the Doctrine of God.* London: Darton, Longman and Todd, 1998.

Swimme, Brian, and Thomas Berry. *The Universe Story.* San Francisco: HarperSanFrancisco, 1992.

Wessels, Cletus. *The Holy Web: Church and the New Universe Story.* Maryknoll, N.Y.: Orbis Books, 2000.

Woods, Richard. *Mysticism and Prophecy: The Dominican Tradition.* London: Darton, Longman and Todd; and Maryknoll, N.Y.: Orbis Books, 1998.

PART 2

Acting Hopefully:
Siding with the Cause of Justice

In a world of evil and suffering, when we say that God is the basis of our hope, this raises inevitable questions about our images of God. What kind of God is the basis of our hope?

Some see God as being the cause of suffering, while others see God as somebody who allows suffering to happen. One of the images that liberation theology has offered is the image of God as one who suffers in and through the victims of injustice. Nolan highlighted this image of God in his writings during the period of apartheid, and it is an image that has the potential of truly making us act hopefully.

For some people the image of a suffering God can escalate their sense of despair and cynicism. How can the basis of our hope be in a God who is suffering in and through the oppressed? For Nolan, this reflects an erroneous notion of God's power. God's power resides not in coercion, control, and domination, but in love and compassion. This image should inspire us to rediscover the power of love and compassion within us. When we begin to see God as being crucified in those who are poor and oppressed, we feel the urge to act hopefully, to be committed to the various activities and campaigns aimed at ending poverty and injustice in our society. In this way, our hope in God, the God who is being crucified in the context of structural injustice, can inspire us to act hopefully.

CHAPTER 4

The Service of the Poor
and Spiritual Growth

Our attitude toward the poor can grow, develop, and mature over the years. On the other hand, it can equally well get stuck, and we can become fixed in our relationship to the people we try to serve. For a Christian this is a matter of spiritual growth. Just as there are stages of prayer and stages of growth in love, and just as St. Bernard can speak of steps in the development of the virtue of humility, so also in our commitment to the poor is there an analogous spiritual experience that goes through different steps or stages with its own crises or dark nights and its own discoveries or illuminations.

This address offers an account of these stages of development. It is an account, of course, based partly on my own experience and partly on the observation of the experience of others. Moreover, this way of dividing the different stages, like any other division of stages of growth, is inevitably stylized and stereotyped. Others may not experience the stages in the same order or in the same manner. This schematization is offered as an aid to understanding what takes place in our common journey toward maturity in the service of the poor.

This is based on an address to the Annual General Meeting of CIIR (Catholic Institute for International Relations, now known as Progressio) in London in June 1984, which CIIR published as a booklet in 1985. The ideas were originally part of a workshop on liberation spirituality given to the Redemptorists in Pokeng, Rustenburg, South Africa, in 1980.

Compassion and Relief Work

The first stage of our commitment to the poor is character-ized by compassion. We have all been moved personally by what we have seen or heard of the sufferings of the poor. Our experience of compassion has been our starting point. But what I am suggesting is that it is only a starting point, and it needs to develop and grow.

Two things help this growth and development of compas-sion. The first is what we have now come to call "exposure." The more we are exposed to the sufferings of the poor, the deeper and more lasting our compassion becomes. Some agen-cies these days organize exposure programs and send people off to a third-world country to enable them to see something of the hardships and misery of grinding poverty. Nothing can replace immediate contact with pain and hunger: seeing people in the cold and rain after their houses have been bulldozed; experiencing the unbearable, intolerable smells in a slum; seeing what children look like when they are suffering from malnutri-tion. But information is also exposure. We know and we want others to know that more than half the world is poor. Some reports indicate that something like 800 million people in the world do not have enough to eat and in one way or another are starving. For many, many people, the only experience of life from the day they are born until the day they die is the experience of being hungry. Information of this kind can help us become more compassionate.

The second thing that seems to me to be necessary to develop our compassion is a willingness to allow it to happen. We can put obstacles in the way of this development by becoming more callous, or saying, "It's not my business," or "I'm in no position to do anything about it." This blunts one's natural compas-sion for the sufferings of the poor. As Christians, however, we have a way of allowing our compassion to develop, a way of nourishing our natural feelings of compassion. We believe that compassion is a virtue, a grace, and indeed a divine attribute. When I experience compassion, I am sharing God's compassion. I am sharing what God feels about the world today. Moreover, my faith enables me to sharpen and deepen my compassion by enabling me to see the face of Christ in those who are suffering and to remember that whatever we do to the least of his brothers and sisters we do to him. That is powerful.

Compassion leads to action. At first our action will probably be what we generally call relief work: collecting and distributing food, blankets, clothes, or money. Compassion for the poor might also lead us to a simplification of our lifestyle: trying to do without luxuries, trying to save money and to give our surplus to the poor. I don't want to go into that. There is nothing extraordinary about it; it is part of a long Christian tradition: compassion, almsgiving, voluntary poverty. Much has been said and written about it.

Compassion, then, would be the primary characteristic of the first stage.

Discovering Structures: The Importance of Anger

The second stage begins with the gradual discovery that poverty is a structural problem. Poverty in the world today is not simply misfortune, bad luck, or inevitable—the result of laziness or ignorance or a lack of development. Poverty in the world today is the direct result of the political and economic policies of governments, political parties, and big business. In other words, the poverty that we have in the world today is not accidental. It has been created; it has been, one almost wants to say, manufactured, by particular policies and systems. Poverty is thus a political problem, a matter of injustice and oppression.

We have seen that the discovery of the depth and breadth of poverty in the world leads to feelings of compassion. So now the discovery that this poverty is being imposed upon people by unjust structures and policies leads to feelings of indignation and anger. We find ourselves getting angry with the rich, with politicians, and with governments. We accuse and blame them for their callousness and inhuman policies.

But our Christian upbringing makes us feel somewhat uncomfortable with anger. We feel a little guilty when we get angry with someone. Is it not sinful to be angry? Should we not be more loving toward the rich? Should we not be forgiving the politicians their sins—seventy times seven times? For those of us who want to continue to follow Christ, our anger and indignation can lead us into a deep spiritual crisis.

The way forward and beyond this crisis is bound up with the discovery of the spiritual importance of God's anger. We all know that there is a great deal about God's anger in the Bible, and not only in the Old Testament. We tend to find this aspect of the Bible rather embarrassing and by no means helpful to our spiritual lives. But maybe it is just here that we have something to learn.

There are two kinds of anger and indignation. One is an expression of hatred and selfishness. The other is an expression of love and compassion. God's anger, indeed his wrath, is an expression of his love for the poor *and* for the rich, for the oppressed *and* for the oppressor. How can that be?

All of us have experienced this kind of anger. When my heart goes out in compassion toward those who suffer, I cannot help feeling angry with those who make them suffer. The deeper my compassion for the poor, the stronger my anger at the rich. The two emotions go together as two sides of the same coin. In fact, I cannot experience the one without the other once I know that the rich exploit the poor. And if I have no feelings of anger, or only very little, then my compassion is simply not serious. My anger is an indication of the seriousness of my compassion, just as God's wrath is a sign of the seriousness of his concern for the poor. Unless I can experience something of God's wrath toward oppressors, my love and service of the poor will not grow and develop.

Yet God's anger does not mean that he has no love for the

rich as persons. We know from experience that we can get angry with the people we love. In fact, our anger can be an expression of the seriousness of our love for them. A mother who discovers her child playing with matches and about to burn down the house must get angry with the child—not because she hates the child but precisely because she loves the child so much. Her anger is an expression of the seriousness of what the child has done and her concern for the child.

Traditionally we distinguish between love of the sinner and hatred of the sin, which is a notoriously difficult thing to do, but the more we understand that the problem is unjust structures rather than individuals who can be held personally responsible for poverty, the easier it is to forgive the individual and hate the system. Individuals are only marginally guilty because they are only vaguely aware, if at all, of what they are doing—like the child playing with matches.

We are all more or less pawns or victims of an unjust system. In South Africa, for example, it is extremely important to recognize that the wickedness of what is happening cannot be blamed upon individuals like P. W. Botha. If he were to be converted, the system and therefore the suffering would continue. If we get angry with P. W. Botha, it is because of the system and the sin he represents rather than because we are able to judge just how guilty he himself might be.

As we grow to share more of God's anger, we find our own anger directed more at unjust systems than at persons, even if this anger is sometimes expressed toward those who represent and perpetuate these systems.

That does not mean that our anger becomes weaker. Our compassion can only develop and mature as we learn to take suffering and oppression seriously enough to get really angry about it.

During this second stage, while we are grappling with the structure and systems that create poverty and while we are learning to share God's anger about them, our actions will be somewhat different from the actions we engaged in during the first stage. We will want to change the system. We will want to engage in certain activities that are calculated to bring about social and political change. Relief work deals with symptoms rather than causes. Relief work is like curative medicine as opposed to preventive medicine. What is the point of trying to relieve suffering while the structures that perpetuate the suffering are left untouched? Preventive action is political action. So we find ourselves participating in social actions, supporting campaigns against governments, and generally getting involved in politics. This approach has its own tensions and constraints, especially if you work for the church or for a funding agency or a research institute. But how else can one serve the poor? Relief work is necessary, but what about preventive work?

Discovering the Strength of the Poor

The third stage of our spiritual development begins with yet another discovery: that the poor must save themselves, will save themselves, and don't really need you or me to save them. Spiritually, this stage is when we come to grips with humility in our service of the poor.

Up to now we will have assumed that we must solve the problems of the poor either by bringing them relief or by changing the structures that oppress them. We think that we, the nonpoor, the educated and conscienticized middle class, the leaders in the church, the people who work for funding agencies and so forth, must come to the rescue of the poor because they themselves are so pitiably helpless and powerless. There may even be some idea of getting them to cooperate with us, or there may be some idea of teaching them to help themselves (the classical theory of development). But it is always "we" who are going to teach "them" to help themselves.

The realization that the poor know better than we do what needs to be done and how to do it may come as a surprise. The further realization that the poor are not only perfectly capable of solving the structural and political problems that beset them but that they alone can do it may shock and shake us. In spiritual terms this can amount to a real crisis for us and to a very deep conversion.

Suddenly we are faced with the need to learn from the poor instead of teaching them. We do not have certain important insights and a certain kind of wisdom precisely because we are so highly educated and precisely because we are not poor and have no experience of what it means to be oppressed. "Blessed are you, Father, for revealing these things not to the learned and the clever but to the little ones" (Matt. 11:25). A considerable amount of humility is needed to listen to and learn from peasants, the working class, and the third world.

When one is dedicated to the service of the poor, accepting that it is not they who need me but I who need them is even more difficult. They can and will save themselves with or without me, but I cannot be liberated without them. In theological terms I have to discover that the poor and oppressed are God's chosen instruments for transforming the world—and not the likes of you and me. God wants to use the poor, in Christ, to save all of us from the madness of a world in which so many people starve in the midst of unimaginable wealth. This discovery can become an experience of God present and acting in the struggles of the poor. Thus, we not only see the face of the suffering Christ in the sufferings of the poor but also hear the voice of God and see the hands of God and his power in the political struggles of the poor.

Having made this discovery and crossed this hurdle, we open ourselves immediately to a particular kind of romanticism: the romanticizing of the poor or the working class or the third world. We Christians seem to have this strange need to romanticize something. Maybe it isn't specific to Christians, but we certainly seem to indulge in it a lot. In the past we tended to romanticize monasticism, and then we had this very romantic idea of the missionary who risks everything to save the souls of pagan savages who live in jungles. We have also tended to romanticize the priesthood, and now we are entering a stage of romanticizing the poor.

We romanticize the poor by putting them on a pedestal and hero-worshiping them. We feel that anything that has been said by someone who is poor and oppressed must be true. We listen to people from the third world as if they possessed some kind of magic, secret knowledge, and whatever the oppressed people of the world do must be right. Any rumor of faults, weaknesses, mistakes, and perversities must be rejected out of hand because the poor are our heroes and heroines. This kind of romanticism does the poor and ourselves no good at all, yet it is extremely difficult to avoid romanticism, at least for a time, during the spiritual development of our service to the poor. What matters is that we do eventually grow out of it.

From Romanticism to Real Solidarity

The fourth and last stage of development begins with the crisis of disillusionment and disappointment with the poor. It begins with the discovery that many poor and oppressed people do have faults, do commit sins, do make mistakes, and do fail us and let us down—or rather fail themselves and sometimes spoil their own cause. The poor are human beings like any of us. They are sometimes selfish, sometimes lacking in commitment and dedication, and sometimes waste money— something that Europeans find particularly irresponsible and incomprehensible. We might even find that some of the poor have more middle-class aspirations than we have and are less conscienticized or politicized than we are.

These discoveries can be an experience of bitter disillusion-ment and profound disappointment, a real crisis or dark night of the soul. But such discoveries can also be the opportunity for a much deeper and more realistic solidarity with the poor, a conversion from romanticism to realism in our service of the poor.

What we need to remember is that the problem of poverty is

a structural one. The poor are not saints and the rich sinners. Individuals cannot be praised for being poor or blamed for being rich, any more than they can be blamed for being poor and praised for being rich. There are exceptions, like those who sell their possessions and embrace voluntary poverty or those who become rich by exploiting the poor knowingly and intentionally. They can be praised and blamed, respectively. But that is not the issue. Most of us find ourselves on one or the other side of the great structural divide of oppressor and oppressed, and this has a profound effect upon the way we think and act. It affects the type of mistakes we are likely to make as well as the type of insights we are likely to have. We can learn from the poor precisely because they are not likely to make the same mistakes that we are likely to make from our position of education and material comfort. Yet the oppression and deprivation that they suffer might lead them to have other misunderstandings and misconceptions. We are all conditioned by our place in the unjust structures of our society. We are all alienated by them. Nevertheless, oppression remains a reality. The two sides are not equal. The poor are the ones who are sinned against and who are suffering. Solidarity with them means taking up their cause, not ours. But we need to do this with them. Together we need to take sides against oppression and unjust structures. Real solidarity begins when it is no longer a matter of "we" and "they." Up to now I have described everything in terms of "we" and "they" because we generally experience the relationship in this manner.

Even when we romanticize the poor and put them on a pedestal we are alienating ourselves from them. Real solidarity begins when we recognize together the advantages and disadvantages of our different social backgrounds and present realities and the quite different roles that we shall therefore have to play while we commit ourselves together to the struggle against oppression. This kind of solidarity, however, must be at the service of a much more fundamental solidarity: the solidarity between the poor themselves. Those who are not poor and oppressed but wish to serve the poor and live in solidarity with them often do so in a manner that divides the poor themselves and sets them one against another. We need to find a way of being part of the solidarity that the poor and oppressed are building with one another. After all, we do all have a common enemy: the system and its injustice.

In the end we will find one another in God—whatever our particular approach to God might be. The system is our common enemy because it is first of all the enemy of God. As Christians we experience this solidarity with one another as a solidarity in Christ, a solidarity with the cause of Christ as the cause of God's justice, which is, in fact, the cause of the poor. It is precisely by recognizing the cause of the poor as God's cause that we can come through the crisis of disillusionment and disappointment with particular poor people.

This ideal is very high, and it would be an illusion to imagine that we could reach it without a long personal struggle that would take us through several stages—crises, dark nights, shocks, and challenges. What matters is that we recognize that we are part of a process. We will always have further to go. We must always remain open to further developments. There are no shortcuts. Moreover, we are not the only ones going through this process. Some will be ahead of us, and we may grapple to understand them. Others will be only beginning on the road to maturity in this matter. We need to appreciate their process, their need to struggle further and grow spiritually. There is no room here for accusations and recriminations. What we all need is encouragement, support, and mutual understanding of the way the Spirit is working in us and through us.

CHAPTER 5

The Option for the Poor in South Africa

"This phrase [the option for the poor] burst upon the ecclesiastical scene only a few years ago. Since then it has become the most controversial religious term since the Reformers' cry, 'salvation by faith alone.'"

These are the opening words of Donal Dorr's recent book on the option for the poor and Vatican social teaching.[1] He is not exaggerating. I should say that the challenge to the church, to almost all our churches, represented by this term "option for the poor" goes far beyond anything envisaged by the Reformers. It challenges both Catholic and Protestant, and it challenges us in a very fundamental way.

In this essay, I should like to do little more than open up the debate about the option for the poor in South Africa. The question has been raised here and there in a variety of forms, mostly without the term "option for the poor"; but in South Africa there has been no systematic Christian practice based upon it and not much research and reflection around this controversial phrase. Dr. Beyers Naudé would be a good example of someone who could be said to have taken this option and

---

This originally appeared in a publication edited by Charles Villa-Vicencio and John de Gruchy titled *Resistance and Hope: South African Essays in Honor of Beyers Naudé*, published in Cape Town by David Philip in 1985. The thinking in this essay, however, has been the subject of many of Nolan's lectures and talks.

[1] Donal Dorr, *Option for the Poor. A Hundred Years of Vatican Social Teaching* (Maryknoll, N.Y.: Orbis Books, 1983).

suffered the consequences, but the biblical grounding and contextual implications of such an option for every Christian in South Africa (black and white, rich and poor) has not been systemically worked out.

My intention, then, is to open up the specific approach implied in this new theological term for further research, reflection, debate, and practice.

A great deal of confusion and misunderstanding exists about the meaning of the phrase itself, and even a measure of deliberate distortion of its meaning. Hence, in the first place, it is necessary to state quite clearly what we are talking about and even more importantly what we are not talking about. Then we have to give some account of how this new theological theme is grounded in the Bible. Finally we must venture some suggestions about what it may mean in the struggle for liberation in South Africa today.

Option for the Poor: What Does It Mean?

One of the most common misunderstandings is that an option for the poor means a choice or preference for preaching and ministering to the poor rather than to the rich. The more recent phrase "preferential option for the poor," made popular by the Puebla Conference of Latin American bishops, has tended to reinforce the idea that all we are talking about is a pastoral preference in the distribution of the church's services, resources, and preaching. We must give more of our attention to the poor and work with them by preference. Some would argue that the church should serve *only* the poor and have nothing whatsoever to do with the rich. Others would respond by saying that the gospel and its message are for all and that we cannot abandon the rich. But all of this misses the point.

The option for the poor is not a choice about the recipients of the gospel message, to whom we must preach the gospel; it is a matter of what gospel we preach to anyone at all. It is concerned with the content of the gospel message itself. The gospel may be good news for the poor and bad news for the rich, but the message is for the poor and the rich.

The opinion that the preferential option for the poor is simply a way of emphasizing the all-importance of almsgiving, charity, and relief work need not delay us here. The poor are not people who are deprived because of bad luck or misfortune. The poor are the oppressed, the victims of the social sin of injustice. The option for the poor is concerned with the sin of oppression and what Christians should be doing about it.[2]

One sometimes hears the objection that the poor are not all saints and the rich are not all sinners. Some people understand their option for the poor in a way that simply romanticizes the poor and imputes guilt to everyone who is not poor. It is thought that anyone who is poor and oppressed is incapable of doing wrong and that anyone who is rich must have knowingly and willingly chosen to make the poor suffer. But this again misses the point. The option for the poor is not a preference for some people over other people. It is a matter of taking up the cause of the poor as opposed to the cause of the rich. The moral judgment involved here is not a judgment about individuals who are rich or poor, but a judgment about the morality or rightness of two conflicting causes. The option for the poor is a judgment about the rightness of the cause of the poor and a condemnation of the cause of the rich, whatever the measure of personal guilt of those involved may or may not be.

It has also sometimes been thought that the option for the poor is a matter of lifestyle: an option for poverty. We do not necessarily help the poor and oppressed by imitating their deprivation. The option for the poor may indeed influence our lifestyle—it may even have a very profound effect upon our material and economic life—but all of this is determined entirely by the exigencies of the struggle for liberation as it is being waged at any particular time.

---

[2]Ibid., 243.

The option for the poor then is an uncompromising and unequivocal taking of sides in a situation of structural conflict. It is not a matter of preaching to some people rather than others, or a matter of being generous to the "underprivileged," or a judgment about the personal guilt of the rich, or even, in the first instance, a matter of lifestyle. It is the assertion that Christian faith entails, for everyone and as part of its essence, the taking of sides in the structural conflict between the oppressor and the oppressed.[3] Nothing could be more threatening to the cherished beliefs of so many of today's Christians. Nothing could be more threatening to so many of our churches in the way they operate in the world today. Nothing could be more controversial and challenging for our theology and our practice as Christians.

Those who feel threatened say that this is not the gospel; it is politics. The gospel, they argue, is about peace and reconciliation, not about taking sides in a conflict. Yes, but surely the gospel does not require us to reconcile good and evil, justice and injustice? Does it not rather demand that we take sides against all sin and especially against the all-pervasive sin of oppression?[4]

These are weighty assertions, though. They call for a solid biblical grounding. In other parts of the world, and by no means only in Latin America, a great deal of biblical research has been done around this topic. We need to be well acquainted with their research as we try to develop our own South African perspective on the poor in the Bible.

The Option for the Poor in the Bible

The option for the poor is not a biblical phrase, but it does sum up very neatly and succinctly one of the most central

---

[3]For the latest account of the Latin American debate on the meaning of the option for the poor, see Gustavo Gutiérrez, *The Power of the Poor in History* (Maryknoll, N.Y.: Orbis Books, 1983).

[4]See Albert Nolan, *Taking Sides* (London: CIIR, 1983).

themes of the Bible. We know that the concept of the poor is central to the whole biblical revelation, but it is so easy to "spiritualize" all that is said about the poor in the Bible by quoting texts that refer to "spiritual poverty" as the attitude of total reliance upon God and having a humble and contrite spirit. There are obvious ulterior motives for this kind of interpretation, but the real point is that what is said in different parts of the Bible about the poor must be interpreted as far as possible in terms of the different historical contexts. Any generalization that ignores the different historical contexts is sure to be arbitrary and biased.

The Option for the Poor in the Exodus Story

The exodus was the original and paradigmatic saving act of God. It was the foundational revelation of Yahweh, the God of the Hebrews. As Rubem Alves puts it, "The exodus was the experience that molded the consciousness of the people of Israel . . . determining the logic with which Israel assimilated the facts of its historical experience and the principle by which it organized them and interpreted them."[5]

The story was told and retold, celebrated each year at the Passover, and used as an interpretative framework for understanding all of God's saving activities, including the death and resurrection of Jesus—the new Passover.[6]

The outline of the exodus story is clear enough. We are introduced to a group of people in Egypt doing forced labor as slaves, building cities and prestigious buildings for the pharaoh (Exod. 1:11). Their cruel oppression and broken spirit (Exod.

---

[5]Quoted in Thomas D. Hanks, *God So Loved the Third World* (Maryknoll, N.Y.: Orbis Books, 1983), 6.

[6]J. Severino Croatto, *Exodus: A Hermeneutics of Freedom* (Maryknoll, N.Y.: Orbis Books, 1981), *passim*; and Alfredo Fierro, *The Militant Gospel: A Critical Introduction to Political Theologies* (Maryknoll, N.Y.: Orbis Books, 1977), 140–51.

6:9) are described at some length. The scene was as common in the ancient world as it is today.

The new thing, the new revelation, was the appearance of a God called Yahweh who actually took notice of them, who saw their oppression, heard their cries, and helped them to escape from their oppressors. Here was a God who actually sided with them rather than, like all other gods, siding with the kings and pharaohs who oppressed them. Later they recognized Yahweh to be the only God, the Creator God, the God of their fathers.

What does this tell us about the option for the poor?

Here we have the original poor people of the Bible, the Hebrew slaves in Egypt. Their poverty is obviously material and economic, but far more striking is that their poverty is the direct result of the structural oppression of Egyptian society. The poor here are the oppressed, and what is described at length is precisely their oppression. Recent studies on the meaning and usage of the Hebrew words for "oppression" have proved beyond any doubt that almost the whole Bible is concerned with the political problem of oppression, and that poverty is seen consistently as the result of oppression.[7]

In the exodus story, the option for these oppressed Hebrews is taken in the first place by Yahweh himself. God takes sides with the oppressed and against the oppressor in no uncertain terms, and this is precisely what counts in Exodus as the fundamental revelation about Yahweh.[8] There is no sense whatsoever in which he can be seen as a God who tries to reconcile or make peace between Pharaoh and his slaves. God rescues or liberates the oppressed from the oppressor, which is what he continues to do throughout the Bible. As we read in Psalm 103:6 (JB), "Yahweh, who does what is right is always on the side of the oppressed."

---

[7]Hanks, *God So Loved*; and Elsa Tamez, *Bible of the Oppressed* (Maryknoll, N.Y.: Orbis Books, 1982).

[8]Fierro, *Militant Gospel*, 140–42; Croatto, *Exodus*, 20.

The other interesting thing about the exodus story is that the poor and oppressed themselves must take an option for their own cause. The work of Moses was precisely to persuade the Hebrew slaves to take up their own cause, which is what faith and trust in Yahweh meant for them in practice.[9] The option for the poor is almost always thought of today as a commitment that the nonpoor have to make to the cause of those who are oppressed, but what is far more fundamental in the Bible is the option of the poor for their own cause. It cannot by any means be taken for granted that all poor people will take up their own cause. Some of them are too broken in spirit and too lacking in hope of success. Others will abandon the cause of the oppressed as a whole in order to promote their own private cause of moving upward into the ranks of the oppressor. This sort of option for the oppressor enables the oppression to continue. The option for the poor is not intended only for those who are not poor and not oppressed.

Of course, in the exodus story Moses himself would be the example of someone who, though not himself oppressed, took sides with the oppressed workers of Egypt.

The Option for the Poor in Canaan

Exodus was only the beginning of the liberation story in the Bible. When the descendants of the Hebrew slaves reached Canaan, they joined forces with oppressed peasants and other rebels, most of whom had a common ancestry. Together they began to build the new nation of Israel. With their background of oppression and with the new hope based upon Yahweh, the liberator of the oppressed, it is not surprising to discover that they built a nation in which there were no rich and no poor; no kings, princes, or even chiefs; and no slaves. It was a federation of twelve tribes, and the land was divided equally among the families or clans (Num. 33:54; 34:18).

---

[9] Tamez, *Bible of the Oppressed*, 60–64.

Recent scholarship has shown beyond doubt that the Israelite society of the twelve tribes was indeed an egalitarian society and that this structure was based upon belief in Yahweh, the liberator of slaves. In this respect, Israel was unique among the nations of the ancient world.[10]

What does this tell us about the option for the poor? Quite clearly, the option that God takes, and which the poor themselves take for their own cause, is an option for an egalitarian society in which there will be no oppressor and no oppressed. The option is not fundamentally for some people and against other people, but an option against all oppression and injustice in favor of a world in which all people benefit from a just freedom and equality.

The Option for the Poor in the Prophets

For reasons that would take too long to explain here, the egalitarian society of the twelve tribes did not last. Gradually inequality set in, despite the attempts of the Jubilee legislation (Lev. 25:8–55) to stem the tide, until eventually the people began to ask for a king in order to be like other nations. The prophet Samuel resisted and warned them that the king and his officials would become rich at their expense and they themselves would become slaves again. But the people insisted and, as the Bible understands it, God allowed them to have a king (1 Sam. 8:1–22).

This was the beginning of oppressive structures within Israel itself. Saul did not become rich, but he proved to be a jealous tyrant. David was a pious and benevolent dictator who began slowly to take on the trappings of an oriental monarch. But Solomon and his successors fulfilled Samuel's worst fears. The majority of the people were reduced to much the same poverty

---

[10]Norman K. Gottwald, *The Tribes of Yahweh: A Sociology of the Religion of Liberated Israel, 1250–1050 B.C.E.* (Maryknoll, N.Y.: Orbis Books, 1979).

and oppression as that from which Yahweh had once liberated them in Egypt and Canaan.

Hence the rise of the great prophets. Although most of the prophets probably did not come from the oppressed classes of Israel, they took up the cause of justice for the poor as Yahweh's cause. The result for almost all the preexilic prophets was persecution, imprisonment, and martyrdom (Matt. 23:29, 33; Luke 6:22, 23, 26). Their identification with the cause of the oppressed led eventually to their own oppression. When Jeremiah himself was hunted and persecuted, he could count himself as one of the poor (Jer. 20:13).

The prophets were almost by definition those who took an option for the oppressed. The kings were almost by definition the oppressors.[11] And it would not be unfair to say that the prophets failed most of all, because the oppressed themselves had not taken an option for their own cause. The result was the destruction of Israel as an independent nation, the deportation of its elite (middle and upper classes) to Babylon (Jer. 29:1–2), and the disappearance of its poor and oppressed classes into the surrounding nations.[12]

The Option for the Poor during and after the Exile

During the centuries after the fall of Jerusalem and the monarchy, in exile in Babylon and after the return to Jerusalem, the remnant of Israel remained a small colony oppressed by a succession of empires: Babylonian, Persian, Greek, and Roman. There was suffering, but on the whole, even in exile, it was not remotely as bad as the oppression experience originally in Egypt. There was a measure of persecution, but now it was

---

[11]J. Kegler, "The Prophetic Discourse and Political Praxis of Jeremiah: Observations on Jer. 26 and 36," in *God of the Lowly, Socio-Historical Interpretations of the Bible*, ed. W. Schottrof and W. Stegemann (Maryknoll, N.Y.: Orbis Books, 1984), 49–54.

[12]B. W. Anderson, *The Living World of the Old Testament*, 3rd ed. (Essex, U.K.: Longman, 1978), 399–400, 404–5, 418.

mostly a religious persecution. With the exception of the Maccabees and later the Zealots, there was no attempt to struggle for liberation. Israel became submissive and opted for a kind of religious independence.

During this period, Israel developed that very special form of Jewish piety that we call "spiritual poverty." The scrolls of the law and of the prophets had been taken into exile by the elite. These they read, interpreted, and rewrote in terms of their present experience.

The poor and oppressed were central to the written tradition they had inherited. The poor were God's favorites. Thus, they read the texts about the poor as applying to themselves, the oppressed remnant of Israel (Zeph. 3:11–13; Isa. 49:13). But now being a member of the remnant of Israel and remaining faithful to Yahweh becomes a matter of personal choice and individual responsibility. And if we also remember that the warnings and condemnations of the prophets made the remnant feel guilty and repentant, we can understand how poverty comes to be thought of as a moral category rather than a social category. To be God's chosen people, the religious remnant of Israel must imitate the "virtues of the poor," which are understood to be the virtues of being humble, meek, contrite, patient, and totally reliant upon God (Isa. 57:15; 66:1–2; Pss. 34:18; 51:17; Mic. 6:6–8; Dan. 3:39; Zeph. 2:3; 3:11–13). To be truly poor becomes a matter of the heart and of the spirit: a humble heart and a contrite spirit.[13]

How does this relate to the option for the poor? The Jews who developed this spirituality of poverty were indeed oppressed, but they regarded themselves alone as the poor of Yahweh. This was the beginning of the detachment of spiritual poverty from its roots in material poverty and in the social category of all the oppressed classes. Instead of taking an op-

---

[13]The most comprehensive, although not the most critical, study of the spiritual poverty of this period available in English is A. Gelin, *The Poor of Yahweh* (Collegeville, Minn.: Liturgical Press, 1964).

tion for the poor, one can then take an option for the virtues of the poor in a way that enables the status quo of oppression to continue unchallenged.

However, some aspects of the piety of the poor that was developed during this period can be of value to us in our commitment to the cause of the poor. Jesus and his movement brought the piety of the poor down to earth again and rooted it firmly in an option for the materially poor and politically oppressed.

The Option for the Poor in the Gospels

In the time of Jesus and his disciples, the remnant of Israel was very conscious of oppression by the Romans. But, like the prophets in previous times, what Jesus draws attention to is the internal structures of oppression. Oppressor and oppressed, rich and poor, could also be found within Jewish society and religion. The Sadducees and the Pharisees, the scribes, the chief priests, and the elders (that is, the nobility and rich landowners) were in various ways oppressors; the poor, the blind, the lame, the crippled, widows and orphans, the sinners, the tax collectors, and prostitutes were all in their own way oppressed people.[14]

In this situation Jesus took sides quite clearly and unequivocally. He spoke of a God who blessed the poor and the oppressed and brought the good news that they would be set free and that God's kingdom belonged to them (Luke 6:20–23; 4:16–22; 12:32).

Jesus' option for the poor included a determined effort to get the poor to take an option for their own cause. He insisted again and again that it was their *faith* that would heal them and save them.[15] He used his position to restore their dignity

---

[14]Albert Nolan, *Jesus before Christianity: The Gospel of Liberation* (London: Darton, Longman, and Todd, 1977), 92–100.

[15]Ibid., 31–36, 41.

and confidence in themselves by telling them that they were "the salt of the earth" and "the light of the world." In short, he told them not to bow down or lie down but to stand up and walk (Luke 17:19; Mark 2:11–12). His preaching of the kingdom gave them hope for the future.

Jesus' option led him to identify himself totally with the poor: "whatever you do to the least of these you do to me" (Matt. 25:40, 45). His stand in favor of the poor and against the oppressor caused, like the prophets, his persecution and eventual death.

There is no way that one could argue that the category of people Jesus was opting for were the morally and spiritually poor. They included sinners, prostitutes, and tax collectors. They included people who were hungry and thirsty and begging on the streets. What moved Jesus to identify with them was not their piety but their suffering.[16] That is not to say that the concept of spiritual poverty is absent in the Gospels. The concept is there. But it is different from the piety of the poor of Yahweh in exilic and postexilic Judaism. The essence of the distinction between material and spiritual poverty in the Gospels has been summed up very simply and concisely by Nicolas Berdyaev: "If I am hungry, that is a material problem; if someone else is hungry, that is a spiritual problem."[17]

The central challenge in the Gospels is the challenge that Jesus presented to the rich and the powerful and to all who had sided with them. He presented them with a simple and uncompromising option: the choice between God and money (Matt. 6:24 par.; compare Mark 4:19 par.). Those who chose God would have to sell their surplus possessions (Matt. 6:19–21; Luke 12:33–34; 14:33) and join with the poor in a sharing community in which no one would be in need (Acts 2:44–46; 4:32, 34–35)—that is to say, where there would be no rich and no poor, no master and no slave. They would not

---

[16]Gutiérrez, *Power of the Poor*, 95, 116, 138, 140–42.
[17]Quoted in ibid., 207.

be poor in the sense of destitute (Greek: *ptochos*), but they would be poor in the sense of having rejected all avarice, greed, and oppression (Greek: *penes*).[18] Or, in Matthew's words, they would "hunger and thirst for justice" (5:6; cf. Luke 6:21); they would not be destitute but they would be "poor in spirit" (5:3; compare Luke 6:20).[19]

Here then is the new spirituality. There is no glorification of poverty but a determination to overcome it. There is no denial that we have enemies but a determination to love them, too (Luke 6:27–35). There is no refusal to recognize the reality of sin in the world but a determination to be forgiving (Matt. 18:21–22). There must be a struggle against all forms of oppression, but there must be no revenge (Matt. 5:38–39).[20]

This would be the spirit of the new community that takes an option against suffering and oppression. It would be sign or symbol of the new Israel, the kingdom that is to come.

The Option for the Poor in South Africa

In our situation of a cruel and relentless oppression that is perpetrated in the name of God and the Bible, it becomes imperative to preach about God as the one who has taken sides, here in South Africa, with all who are oppressed—and to preach this to everyone. It will then be necessary to spell out, work out, and live out the consequences of this for the various groups among the oppressed and the oppressing or exploiting classes.

The oppressed must take a clear option for their own cause, for the cause of all the poor and oppressed. An option

---

[18]See the interesting study on the meaning of the word for poverty in the New Testament by Wolfgang Stegemann, *The Gospel and the Poor* (Philadelphia: Fortress, 1984), 13–21, 33–53.

[19]Hanks, *God So Loved*, 11; Gustavo Gutiérrez, *A Theology of Liberation* (Maryknoll, N.Y.: Orbis Books, 1973), 290, 299–302.

[20]See the interesting approach of G. Theissen to the spirituality of the Jesus movement. *The First Followers of Jesus: Sociological Analysis of the Earliest Christianity* (London: SCM, 1978), 99–110.

to become upwardly mobile by oneself or with a small group that abandons the rest of the oppressed is not an option for the poor but an option to join the oppressing and exploiting classes. People in South Africa are oppressed in many different ways and to different degrees. Workers are oppressed, some much more than others; blacks are oppressed, but some suffer considerably more than others; women are oppressed, but not all to anything like the same extent. It becomes possible, therefore, to be oppressed on one account while being part of the oppression on another account. An option for the poor is an option against every form of oppression and exploitation. An analysis of the relationship between the various forms of oppression is helpful here. But a Christianity that does not challenge the poor and oppressed themselves, including women, to take an option and join in the struggle for liberation is simply unbiblical.

Many of the churches in South Africa, especially through their official statements and sometimes in Sunday sermons, are beginning to take a prophetic stance. But in view of what we have seen of the option for the poor in the Bible, we may well ask whether the stance of these churches has gone nearly far enough. There is a growing denunciation of injustice, but no clear annunciation of hope for a future liberated society. There are challenges to the government and to whites in general, but no clear statement that the oppressed should take up their own cause as God's cause. The stance of the churches is not clear. If whites are supposed to take an option against oppression, what does this mean in practice? Not many of them are likely to want to take an option for the poor, but what do we say to those who do want to do so?

Those who profess a willingness to side with the oppressed in South Africa will have much to learn. It is obvious that siding with the poor is easier said than done. A purely theoretical decision that apartheid is heretical and sinful is not enough.

In religious terms, what is required is a deep conversion, an experience of being born again, and a long spiritual journey. Before one's option for the poor can become a truly practical reality, there are ingrained prejudices to be overcome as well as other emotional and cultural obstacles.

One of the more serious emotional obstacles is based upon the fact that we do not experience the same daily sufferings and insecurities as the poor. When you are not humiliated at every turn and regularly beaten up by the police, you do not experience the same emotions of fear, frustration, anger, and indignation. You may side with the oppressed, but you will not easily feel the same way about the oppressor, and that makes it more difficult to share God's anger at what is happening daily in our country. However, as we get involved in a practical way and as we begin to risk our own security and comfort, our reputation, and even our lives, a certain sharing of the experience of oppression and of God's anger becomes possible.

Then there are the cultural obstacles. It may be that a new culture is being born within the struggle for liberation in South Africa, but at present we have to face the fact of cultural differences and try to transcend them as part of our option. The cultural differences are not merely African and Western. There are also cultural differences between the working class and the middle class of any race, between youth culture and adult culture, and between people of various backgrounds: Afrikaners, Indians, Portuguese. These differences are not significant, and they can easily be overcome by people who have taken the same option, but there is no value in pretending that they do not even exist.[21]

Taking an option for the poor is like setting out on a new

---

[21]B. Tlhagale, "Transracial Communication," in *Missionalia,* 11, no. 3 (1983): 113–23.

spiritual journey.[22] It is so easy to get stuck along the way, at the liberal stage of paternalism or at the romantic stage of glorifying the poor. It is so easy to think that one has all the answers because of one's superior education or analysis. A thoroughgoing option for the poor includes the willingness to question one's assumptions and to learn from those who are oppressed. Only after one has learned to have confidence in the ability of the oppressed to promote their own cause and bring about their own liberation can one begin to share that struggle with them and to make a contribution in real solidarity with all those who have taken an option against oppression.

Centuries of apartheid or racial capitalism have left their mark upon all classes and groups in South Africa. Only the self-righteous will claim to be immune. We need to be redeemed, liberated, and cleansed.

What I am suggesting is that we might try to do this by exploring together in practice, study, and research a common option taken by all classes and races for all the oppressed. The term "option for the poor" itself does not matter. We might choose to call it something else. What matters is the uncompromising commitment to the cause of the oppressed as the cause of God.

---

[22]See the spiritual journey in Gustavo Gutiérrez, *We Drink from Our Own Wells: The Spiritual Journey of a People* (Maryknoll, N.Y.: Orbis Books, 1984), *passim*.

CHAPTER 6

Taking Sides

We live today in a world of conflict: between governments and peace movements, between trade unions and employers, between feminists and male-dominated institutions. In El Salvador and Guatemala, conflicts between the rich and the poor cost countless lives. In South Africa, the situation has been described as a total conflict, and military chiefs have called it total war.

There may be differences of opinion about the nature of a particular conflict, whether it is a racial conflict or a class conflict, or whether the conflict might be resolved by peaceful negotiation rather than the use of force. But for many people in the world, the fact of a conflict, which may encompass every aspect of their lives, can hardly be doubted.

Taking Sides

This situation of conflict poses very important questions for us as Christians. What should be our attitude to the conflicts in which we find ourselves and that we see around us? Should we take sides, or must we always remain neutral?

From the start we should make clear that these questions are distinct from the question of using or not using violence.

This first appeared in print in a booklet published by the Catholic Truth Society and the CIIR in London in 1985. It has since been published in many places and languages.

People in Northern Ireland, for example, may hope fervently for a united Ireland or for continued union with Britain—they may, in other words, "take sides"—while rejecting the use of violence to achieve it. We are not in this essay discussing the question of whether or not there are occasions when the use of violence in pursuit of justice is justified. In countries like El Salvador, Guatemala, and South Africa, it is often almost impossible to disentangle the question of taking sides and the question of violence, but these questions are nonetheless separate and need to be talked about quite separately in the light of the gospel.

To many of us, there are obviously some conflicts in which we ought to take sides. But what about the Christian belief in reconciliation, forgiveness, and peace? How can you take sides if you love everybody, including your enemies? And how do we account for the widespread belief that in any conflict a Christian should be a peacemaker who avoids taking sides and tries to bring about a reconciliation between the opposing forces?

This belief rests on a mistaken understanding of reconciliation. We have all heard people say, We must be fair, we must listen to both sides of the story; there is always right and wrong on both sides. If we could only get people to talk to one another to sort out their misunderstandings and misconceptions of one another, the conflict could be resolved. On the face of it this sounds very Christian. It sounds like a genuine concern for fairness and justice.

Three Common Mistakes

So what is wrong with this argument?

In the first place it makes reconciliation an absolute principle that must be applied in all cases of conflict. The model or example that it envisages is that of what one might call the "private quarrel" between two people who are being argumentative and not trying to understand one another and whose differences are based upon misunderstandings. But not all conflicts are like this. In some conflicts one side is right and the other wrong; one side is being unjust and oppressive, and the other is suffering injustice and oppression. In such cases, a policy of seeking consensus and not taking sides would be quite wrong. Christians are not supposed to try to reconcile good and evil, justice and injustice; we are supposed to do away with evil, injustice, and sin.

The first mistake, then, is the assumption that all conflicts are based upon misunderstandings and that blame always exists on both sides. No evidence is present for believing that this is always the case, either in conflicts between individuals or in conflicts between groups in society. The assumption is unfounded and has nothing whatsoever to do with Christianity. This assumption could only be made by people who do not suffer under injustice and oppression or who do not really appreciate the sinfulness and evil of what is happening.

The second mistake in this argument is that it assumes that a person can be neutral in all cases of conflict. In fact, neutrality is not always possible, and in cases of conflict due to injustice and oppression, neutrality is totally impossible. If we do not take sides with the oppressed, then we are, albeit unintentionally, taking sides with the oppressor. Bringing the two sides together in such cases is actually extremely beneficial to the oppressor, because it enables the status quo to be maintained; it hides the true nature of the conflict, keeps the oppressed quiet and passive, and brings about a kind of pseudo-reconciliation with justice. The injustice continues, and everybody is made to feel that the injustice doesn't matter because the tension and conflict have been reduced.

This brings us to the third mistake. The commonly held view that Christians should always seek harmony and a middle way in every dispute assumes that tension and conflict are worse evils than injustice and oppression. This false supposition is again based upon a lack of compassion for those who suffer under oppression. Those people who are afraid of conflict or confrontation, even when it is nonviolent, are usually those who are not convinced of the need for change. Their caution hides an unchristian pessimism about the future, a lack of hope. Or they use the Christian concern for reconciliation to justify a form of escapism from the realities of injustice and conflict.

All in all, these mistakes about Christian reconciliation are not simply a matter of misunderstandings but come from a lack of real love and compassion for those who are suffering, or from a lack of appreciation of what is really happening in a grave conflict. In the final analysis, the insistent pursuit of an illusory neutrality in every conflict is a way of siding with the oppressor.

True Reconciliation

What then is the meaning of reconciliation? What does reconciliation mean in the Bible?

The history of the Jewish people in the Bible is very much a history of conflict with the pagan nations. This conflict and confrontation are not merely encouraged by God; he actually commands the people again and again to oppose the tyranny, injustice, and immorality of the pagan nations. One of the greatest sins of the Jewish nation was their attempt to be reconciled with the pagan nations who oppressed them. When the people shouted "Peace, peace," Jeremiah responded by saying there is no peace and never can be peace without change or conversion.

Some people today ignore this statement; they say that the New Testament is different in that Jesus brought a message of peace and reconciliation. Of course, one of the things that Jesus wished to hand on to his disciples was his peace, and he said, "Blessed are the peacemakers," but this statement must be understood in the context of the much more remarkable saying we inherit from Jesus in the Gospels of Matthew and Luke.

"Do you suppose that I am here to bring peace on earth?"

(The question is interesting. It seems to suggest that some people did suppose that Jesus had come to bring peace on earth.) "No, I tell you, but rather dissension. For from now on a household will be divided: three against two, and two against three: the father divided against the son, son against father, mother against daughter, daughter against mother: mother-in-law against daughter-in-law, daughter-in-law against mother-in-law" (Luke 12:51–53; Matt. 10:34–36). Most of this is a quotation from the prophet Micah (7:6), who was deploring the conflict between parents and children. Jesus used the quote to say that this is just the kind of conflict and dissension that he will bring. And, of course, this is exactly what he did do—not because he wanted to bring dissension and conflict for their own sake, but because his uncompromising stance inevitably divided the people into those who were for him and those who were against him.

Moreover, in the already existing conflict between Pharisees and the so-called sinners, he sided with the sinners, prostitutes, and tax collectors against the Pharisees. In the conflict between the rich and the poor, he sided with the poor. Jesus did not treat each side as equally right or equally wrong, or only needing to overcome their misunderstandings about one another. He condemns the Pharisees and the rich in no uncertain terms, and he forgives the sinners and blesses the poor. In fact, he enters right into the conflict with the Pharisees and the rich to such an extent that they set out to discredit him, arrest him, charge him, and execute him. Jesus makes no attempt to compromise with the authorities for the sake of a false peace or reconciliation or unity.

On the other hand, Jesus at times does try to reconcile people who have been in conflict with one another—for example, Jews and Samaritans, Zealots and tax collectors, some individual Pharisees and sinners or the poor, and so on. Probably for this reason he was known as a man of peace.

But how is one to reconcile these two apparently contradictory approaches to conflict? Jesus made a distinction between the peace that God wants and the peace that the world wants (John 14:27). The peace that God wants is a peace based on the truth, justice, and love. The peace that the world offers us is a superficial peace and unity that compromises the truth, that covers over the injustices, and that is usually settled on for thoroughly selfish purposes. Jesus destroys this false peace and even highlights the conflicts in order to promote a true and lasting peace. There is no question of preserving peace and unity at all costs, even at the cost of truth and justice. Rather it is a matter of promoting truth and justice at all costs, even at the cost of creating conflict and dissension along the way. Thomas Aquinas makes this same point by distinguishing between peace and concord, pointing out that concord is possible between thieves and murderers but that true peace is based upon genuine love.

Different Kinds of Conflict

We noted before that there are different kinds of conflict. We must analyze each situation and respond accordingly. If one side is right, we must recognize this and side with them. If the other side is wrong and in power, we must oppose them and dethrone them from power. Furthermore we must analyze the reasons for the conflict, the interests that are at stake, and the dynamics of change through conflict. The idea that all one has to do is talk nicely to both sides and they will be reconciled is simply not true in most cases of conflict, especially conflicts between groups or interests rather than individuals. Social forces are often at play that make change and conflict much more difficult and complicated than that.

On the other hand, we may discover that both sides are basically right, that both sides are working for justice. In such cases, reconciliation is very important in order to create a cooperative solidarity in the struggle against injustice. And if we discover that both sides are wrong and that both are part of the oppression, then both must be confronted. Then, obviously, we don't try to reconcile them in their differences about the most effective way to oppress others.

Structural Conflict

To get to the real root of many conflicts, we have to begin to think in structural terms—in other words, that not just individuals may be right or wrong, but the way that societies are structured may itself be right or wrong. In some cases, a structural conflict is present between the oppressor and the oppressed, between the rich and the poor. The squabble is not personal. In these cases, we cannot and should not impute guilt to the individuals concerned, nor should we treat everyone on the one side as blameless and everyone on the other side as guilty. Structurally, the cause of the poor and the oppressed is right and just, no matter what individual poor people may be like in their personal and private lives. Structurally, the cause of the rich and oppressor is wrong, no matter how honest and sincere and unaware they may be.

Thus, in the Magnificat or Song of Mary in the Gospel of Luke, Mary says that it is God who "pulls down the mighty from their thrones and exalts the lowly, who fills the hungry with good things and sends the rich away empty" (Luke 1:52–53). This statement does not mean that God hates the rich and the powerful and that he wants to destroy them as people. It simply means that he wants to pull the rich and powerful from their thrones, from their position in society, because the structures of that society are unjust and oppressive.

This is the sense in which we must be on the side of the poor if we want to be on God's side. We must take an option for the poor, for the sake of both the poor and the rich as individual people. In fact, within this situation of structural conflict, the only way to love everyone is to side with the poor and the oppressed. Anything else is simply a way of siding with oppression and injustice.

Loving Our Enemies

This brings us to the question of loving our enemies. Here we must first point out that the commandment to love one's enemies only makes sense once we recognize that we do have enemies, and that they are really and truly our enemies. When people hate you and curse you and oppress you, Jesus does not say that you must pretend that they are not your enemies. They are. And when he says you must love them despite this, he does not mean that you must avoid any conflict or confrontation with them.

Confrontation and conflict do not, and need not necessarily, entail hatred. Class conflict and class struggle, which Christians have traditionally been reluctant to acknowledge, do not necessarily entail hatred. Such struggles may in fact be the only effective way of changing the situation, the only effective way of pulling down the mighty from their thrones.

Those people and institutions that maintain an unjust distribution of wealth and power and those who prop up their thrones are in fact our enemies. They are everybody's enemies; they are even the enemies of their own humanity. As a group or class they will never come down from their thrones willingly or voluntarily. A few individuals here and there may do so, but there will always be others to replace them. The ruling class as a whole cannot step down: we will have to pull them down from their thrones—not in order to sit on those thrones ourselves, or to put others on them, but in order to destroy thrones.

The temptation for a Christian is to think that the most loving thing to do is to convert one by one those who sit on the thrones of injustice and thus to destroy the system. But change does not happen that way, because as long as the throne remains it will always be filled by others and the oppression will remain. The only effective way of loving our enemies is to engage in action that will destroy the system that makes them our enemies. In other words, for the sake of love and for the sake of true peace, we must side with the poor and the oppressed and confront the rich and powerful, and join the conflict or struggle against them—or rather against what they stand for and what they are defending.

In countries marked by grave injustice, joining the conflict—not judging it from a distance—is the only effective way of bringing about the peace that God wants.

In countries possessing nuclear weapons, there may be no shortcut around conflict with governments if the world is to progress toward disarmament. It is not possible to balance or reconcile the needs of the 40 million people who die from starvation each year in the third world with the needs of arms manufacturers and military strategists or the demands of a few wealthy nations to be able to destroy any potential attacker many times over. Decisions have to be made; one has to take sides.

PART 3

Putting God into the Picture

As the struggle against injustice goes on, seemingly with no sign of victory in sight, persevering in hope is often difficult. The attitude of hopefulness is therefore tied to time. Those engaged in the struggle ask when the victory shall come about. They ask, "Victory is certain but can we really say that it is near? The struggle has been going on for such a long time. Is it not likely to drag on for many more years?" (Nolan 1988, 182). From a religious point of view, they ask about the time for liberation and salvation: "When will salvation come for us? Must we wait until the next life? Must we wait until the last day?" (Nolan 1988, 117). When they do not receive adequate answers, their sense of hope sometimes transforms into despair and cynicism.

Nolan thinks we need prophets who can assist us in answering such questions, for prophets are people driven by the spirit of God to tell the time. "In the Bible, the prophet was someone who could tell the time. He (or she) could see what kind of time it was and what kind of action would be appropriate now. The prophets could read the signs of the times, which means they could interpret the kairos, interpret the signs that would indicate what kind of time it was" (Nolan 1986d, 132).

The prophets do not simply determine what kind of time it is; they bring God into the picture. When the prophets put

73

God into the picture, they are then able to tell the type of time the society is living in. Is it an ordinary moment? Is it a kairos moment? Or is it an eschaton moment? In an article that he wrote in 1996, Nolan describes how the authors of the Kairos Document inserted God into the picture and announced the type of moment through which South Africa was passing. The authors of this document (of which Nolan was one) announced the kairos moment in South Africa, a special moment in history, a moment of grace, a moment that signaled an urgent need for a decisive action in the struggle against apartheid. "It is at times like this that God visits the people, that God walks down our streets and enters right into our homes. Everyday life is turned upside down and inside out and nothing will ever be the same again. These are the favorable times, the times of grace when God offers us the kind of opportunity that our predecessors might have longed to see but never saw" (Nolan 1986d, 135).

Prophets are valuable in our society, not only for their role of announcing the kairos moment, but also for inspiring hope even in ordinary moments, where God is equally at work. In some ways, we can discover such prophets within ourselves if we are open to the spirit of God, who blows wherever she wills. With such an openness we are able to feel the same way as God about events that are happening in society. One is able to share God's anger, God's compassion, God's sorrow, God's disappointment, God's revulsion, God's sensitivity for people, and God's seriousness. Through such empathy a prophet is then able to read the signs of the times and discern what God is saying and doing in and through the events of history. Only then can we put God into the picture.

CHAPTER 7

Theology in a Prophetic Mode

It is not without reason that Archbishop Tutu has been hailed throughout the world as a modern-day prophet. His sermons, talks, and many public statements can be aptly described as theology in a prophetic mode. What does this mean? What are the characteristics of a prophetic theology, and what does it imply for South Africa at this moment of its history?

Attempting a comprehensive outline of prophetic theology in this brief essay would not be possible. However, a fundamental characteristic of this mode in theology underlies everything else and distinguishes it from every other theology or mode of theology: the characteristic of being *time-bound*. All prophecy and prophetic theology speaks of, and speaks to, a particular time in a particular place about a particular situation. I would like to examine in this essay this aspect of theology in a prophetic mode.

The Kairos Document has drawn our attention quite recently to the theological significance of a particular moment in history, a crisis, a *kairos*—and the document has nailed it down to the particular crisis in which South Africa finds itself today. This alone would make the theology of the Kairos Document prophetic in character or mode. But unfortunately

This was first published in *Hammering Swords into Ploughshares: Essays in Honor of Archbishop Mpilo Desmond Tutu*, ed. B. Tlhagale and I. Mosala (Grand Rapids: Eerdmans, 1986), and then in *The Future of Liberation Theology: Essays in Honor of Gustavo Gutiérrez*, ed. Marc Ellis and Otto Maduro (Maryknoll, N.Y.: Orbis Books, 1989).

the document devotes no more than a page and a half to this all-important notion of a *kairos* or moment of truth. Much more needs to be said if theology in a prophetic mode is to be taken up and developed fully, effectively, and powerfully in South Africa. Moreover, that this path of investigation would also be one of the ways of liberating ourselves from the dominant Western world that still imprisons and entombs our theology in South Africa is no mere coincidence. Western theology is singularly unprophetic because it understands all truth to be timeless and universal. This understanding, among other things, became a very convenient tool for colonizing the minds of much of the human race and for excluding all possibility of prophetic thinking. The biblical prophets were far removed from our Western intellectuals in many ways, including the fact that their message was *not* timeless and universal.

Gerhard von Rad, after many years of research on the message of the prophets, draws this conclusion:

> It is all important not to read this message as if it consisted of timeless ideas, but to understand it as the particular word relevant to a particular hour in history, which therefore cannot be replaced by any other word. The prophetic word never tries to climb into the realm of general religious truth, but instead uses even the most suspect means to tie the listening partner down to his [sic] particular time and place in order to make him understand his own situation before God.[1]

A typically non-Western way of conceiving time exists that is not only Hebrew and biblical but also, in at least some way, African. The Western concept of time, however, has been part and parcel of our education in South Africa as elsewhere. And it has its uses. But to speak theologically and prophetically about

---

[1]*The Message of the Prophets* (London: SCM Press, 1968), 100.

a particular moment of time without going beyond the Western concept of chronological time would not be possible.

The simplest and briefest way of making this clear and of developing a basis for a prophetic theology in South Africa today would be to make a clear distinction between three kinds of time. The three kinds of time might best be designated by the three Greek words *chronos*, *kairos*, and *eschaton*.

Chronos

Chronos is the typically Western concept of time. *Chronos* means time as a measurement: the time of measured hours and dates, the time that is recorded on clocks and calendars. A historical epoch in this way of thinking is identified by the date it began and the date it ended. Time is conceived of as a measured and numbered empty space that can be filled with events of greater or lesser importance. *Chronos* is what one might call *quantified time*.

This concept is what comes to mind immediately and almost exclusively in Western thinking when the word "time" is mentioned: a quantified measurement. However, *chronos* is not the way the Bible thinks of time. In the words of von Rad, "Today one of the few things of which we can be quite sure is that this concept of absolute time, independent of events, and, like blanks on a questionnaire, only headings to be filled up with data which will give it (time) content, was unknown to Israel."[2]

Kairos

Kairos, on the other hand, refers to time as a quality. A particular *kairos* is the particular quality or mood of an event. This concept is clearly and succinctly expressed in the well-known passage from Ecclesiastes (3:1–8):

---

[2]Ibid., 77.

There is a time for everything;
A time for giving birth
A time for dying
A time for planting
A time for uprooting
A time for killing
A time for healing
A time for knocking down
A time for building
A time for tears
A time for laughter
A time for mourning
A time for dancing
A time for loving
A time for hating
A time for war
A time for peace.

For the Hebrew, to know the time was not a matter of knowing the hour or the date; it was a matter of knowing what kind of time it was. Was it a time for tears or a time for laughter, a time for war or a time for peace? To misjudge the time in which one was living must be disastrous. To continue to mourn and fast during a time of blessing would be like sowing during harvest time (see Zech. 7:1–3). Time here is the quality or mood of events.

This concept of time is not entirely foreign to us. It is particularly meaningful to those who inherit an African culture and even more meaningful when we are involved in an intensified struggle to change the times. We know about times of mourning that make it inappropriate to celebrate a joyful Christmas. We have discussed whether it is a time for boycotting or a time for returning to school. There is a time for conflict and confrontation and a time for reconciliation and peace, but unfortunately we do not relate each different *kairos* to God as easily and as naturally as the people of the Bible did. This indeed is where prophetic theology comes in and where we have much to learn from the Bible.

In the Bible the prophet was someone who could tell the time. He (or she) could see what kind of time it was and what kind of action would be appropriate now. The prophets could read the signs of the times, which means they could interpret the *kairos*, interpret the signs that would indicate what kind of time it was (compare Matt. 16:3 with Luke 12:56).

Prophecy, however, was not just a matter of knowing one's *kairos;* it was also a matter of finding God in it. For the prophets, God determined the different times, and therefore it is God who speaks to us and challenges us through our particular *kairos*. Revelation has a tremendous immediacy here. God is directly involved in the changing times. God speaks loudly and clearly through this crisis or that conflict or some victory over the forces of evil. Theology in a prophetic mode is a theology that can find and experience God as alive and active in the excitement or the sadness or the suffering of our present *kairos*. This is not to say that every moment of chronological time is equally important or significant and that God can be found equally in every and any event. Every event in history is not a *kairos*. A divine *kairos* is a very special and significant time. There are lulls in history when nothing of significance happens. For the Bible, such chronological times are simply not history. History is the succession of God-inspiring events. The gift of the prophet is the ability to recognize such events, such critical times, and to spell them out as moments of truth, as challenges, as opportunities, as times for decision and action. A *kairos* is a privileged time in which not everyone is called to witness or participate. Such was, of course, the time of Jesus, which is why he could say to his disciples: "Happy the eyes that see what you see, for I tell you that many prophets and kings wanted to see what you see and never saw it" (Luke 10:23–24). The time of Jesus was of course a unique and unrepeatable *kairos*, but that does not mean that there can be no other specially privileged times. Today in South Africa, according to the prophetic theology of the Kairos Document, is indeed for us an unprecedented *kairos*.

At times like this, God visits the people. God walks down our streets and enters right into our homes. Everyday life is turned upside down and inside out, and nothing will ever be the same again. These times are the favorable times, the times of grace when God offers us the kind of opportunity that our predecessors might have longed to see but never saw, and woe betide us if we do not rise to the challenge.

But even this is not all. The real specialness and seriousness of a prophetic *kairos* is determined by its relationship to another kind of time: the *eschaton*.

Eschaton

Eschatological time or the *eschaton* is a notoriously difficult concept. Biblical scholars crack their heads over it and come up with a whole range of different theories from realized eschatology to consistent eschatology and existential eschatology. I have no intention of delving into these theories, because I think that the present crisis in South Africa can provide us with a simple and practical appreciation of what the prophets had in mind.

Put quite simply, an *eschaton* is an event of the near future, an act of God, that determines the quality, the mood, and the seriousness of our present time—that is to say, it turns the present moment into a particular kind of *kairos*. This way of thinking about God and time requires some unpacking.

A very important characteristic of all prophetic thinking is that it turns the attention of the people from the past to the future. Prophets are called prophets precisely because they speak about the future. Instead of trying to understand the present in terms of the events of the past (for example, Exodus, Mount Sinai, or King David), the prophets ask the people to think of the present time in terms of a future act of God. They challenge the people to break with the past and to look forward to something new: "Remember not the former things," says God in Isaiah, "I am going to do a new thing" (43:18–19).

An *eschaton* is a qualitatively and radically new event. Notice how often the prophets use the word "new": the new covenant, the new age, a new heart, a new spirit, the new heaven and new earth, the new Jerusalem, or simply the fact that God is going to do a new thing. Prophets look forward to a future in which new and unprecedented things will happen, and even when they looked back to the past and the traditions of the past they would interpret them anew in view of the new future. Thus, the covenant makes prophets think of the new covenant to come; the exodus turns their attention to the new exodus, Jerusalem to the new Jerusalem, and so forth.

The prophets did not use the Greek word *eschaton*. When they spoke of the new future, they called it "the day of Yahweh," "the day of vengeance," "the latter days," "the days that are coming," or simply "the day." At a later stage the *eschaton* was referred to as "the coming of the new age," and Jesus makes use of the same idea when he speaks of "the coming of the kingdom of God."

The first and most important thing that Jesus and all the prophets have to say about this new future or *eschaton* is that it is "near," "at hand," "coming soon." The prophets stand up to make the momentous announcement that "the day of Yahweh is near." (See, for example, Isa. 13:6, 9; Jer. 46:10; Ezek. 7:7, 12; 30:3; Joel 1:15; 4:14; Zeph. 1:7; Zech. 14:1.) Jesus comes to proclaim that "the kingdom of God is near" (Matt. 4:17 and par.). Of course they are not all referring to the same day, nor are they all speaking about the last day. The *eschaton* is a new saving act of God that was imminent or near for them at that time.

The new saving act of God that will happen on the day of Yahweh is an act of judgment and salvation. Not that they have in mind what we call the last judgment or eternal salvation. They have in mind a particular day or time when God will punish those who are presently doing evil and save or vindicate or liberate those who are now enslaved or in exile or suffering oppression. The Hebrew verb "to judge" means literally "to put right what is wrong." We can say then that the *eschaton* is an event of the near future in which God is going to put right all that is presently wrong. That will mean punishment for those who are doing wrong and salvation for those who are being wronged.

In the minds of the Old Testament prophets, this future event will take the form of a mighty war[3] in which the forces of evil will be destroyed so that peace and justice may reign on earth. Many of the prophets give vivid and terrifying descriptions of this mighty war of liberation. For but a few examples, one can read about the imminent destruction of Babylon and Edom in Isaiah 13 and 34 and the terrifying massacre of the Egyptians by the Babylonians in Jeremiah 46:1–24 and Ezekiel 30, not to mention the many descriptions of the slaughter of the Jewish ruling class in Jerusalem on the day of Yahweh because of all their sins (see, for example, Joel 2:1–11 and Ezek. 37).

The prophets found no pleasure in describing all this horrific bloodshed. They trembled and shuddered at the very thought of it, and they describe with great compassion the fear and suffering of so many of the people. Theirs is not a dispassionate and objective description of a war, but a prophetic warning about a world-shaking event that will be experienced as a cosmic upheaval:

> The earth quakes, the skies tremble,
> sun and moon grow dark,
> the stars lose their brilliance. (Joel 2:10)

We know this apocalyptic type of description of a cosmic upheaval, and we come across it again in the Gospels (for example, Mark 13:24–25). The experience of a terrible war fundamentally changes the face of the earth and is a turning point in human history. It is an *eschaton*.

---

[3]Ibid., 95ff.

But the day of Yahweh is not only a day of vengeance, a time of gloom and doom. The prophets were in no doubt about the terrifying seriousness of what was going to happen, the awful seriousness of God's anger. But they never lost hope. On the contrary, the peace, the salvation, the justice, and the equality that they were always hoping for would be the outcome of these very wars and upheavals. They have equally vivid descriptions of the peace and happiness that God will bring: when the lion lies down with the lamb (Isa. 11:6–9; 65:25) and swords are melted into plowshares (Isa. 2:2–5; Mic. 4:1–5), when there will be nothing more to fear (Zeph. 3:13), and peace and justice will reign supreme (Isa. 32:16–17) because the law will be written in the hearts of the people (Jer. 31:33) and the Spirit of God will be in them (Exod. 36:26). On that day God will put right all that is now wrong. The oppressors will be destroyed or converted, and the poor and oppressed will live in peace (Zeph. 3).[4]

This same idea of an *eschaton* appears in the New Testament when Jesus speaks about the coming of wars and rumors of wars (Mark 13) and the destruction of Jerusalem (Luke 19:43–44; 21:20–23; 23:28), which he speaks of as the birth pangs of God's kingdom (Mark 13:8).

However, for Jesus and the prophets the destructive side of the *eschaton*, the bloodshed, is not inevitable and absolutely unavoidable. As far as the Jewish prophets were concerned, there was probably very little, if anything, that they could do about the massacre of the Egyptians by the Babylonians or later of the Babylonians by the Medes except to see that it would be to the advantage of Israel. But when the Israelites themselves, or at least their ruling class, are the oppressors, then at least the prophets can appeal to them in the name of Yahweh to change their ways before they are destroyed. This

---

[4]Norbert Lohfink, "Zefania und das Israel der Armen," *Bibel arid Kirche* 3, no. 3 (1984): 100–108, summarized in *Theology Digest* 32, no. 2 (1985): 113–24.

is where Jesus and the prophets' oft-repeated call to repentance and conversion comes in, the element of *metanoia*, and this is what constitutes their present moment as a special divine *kairos*, a moment of truth.

A *kairos* is a moment of grace, a unique opportunity precisely because the *eschaton* or day of reckoning is near. A *kairos* is a time for decision and action, a time for oppressors and wrongdoers to be converted. At the same time, the *kairos* is a time for rejoicing and for hope because the *eschaton* as the day of liberation is near at hand—whether the oppressor is converted or not, whether there will be bloodshed or not. The element of hopefulness and expectancy in any genuine *kairos* should not be overlooked. It is indeed one of the constitutive elements of a divine *kairos*.

The fundamental insight of prophetic theology, then, is the recognition that an *eschaton* or day of reckoning and liberation is near, which turns the present moment into a *kairos*. Everything else in prophetic theology follows from here. But one may well ask how anyone can be sure that an eschatological event is close at hand or how the prophets themselves could have known when their *eschaton* would occur.

Here again we would first need to be reminded that the nearness of an *eschaton* is not a matter of *chronos* or measured time. In other words, a prophet would not be able to tell you the day or the hour when all these things will happen. Jesus makes this quite clear when he says that nobody, not even he himself, knows the day or the hour (Mark 13:32 and par.). But the impossibility of pinning the *eschaton* down to a chronological date did not make Jesus or the prophets any less certain about the central truth that their *eschaton* was near. What they are speaking about, then, is another kind of time relationship, the extremely close relationship between the present *kairos* and a future *eschaton*. In fact, qualitatively speaking, the two events are so bound up together that they are almost contemporaneous. The *eschaton* is the event that determines and qualifies, or should determine and qualify, the whole mood and atmosphere of the present time.[5] If we believe that war, revolution, liberation, or any other total upheaval is imminent, this belief will color our whole understanding of our present reality. Once we realize that something totally new is about to happen, we are already living in a new time. Or if we come to believe that the day of reckoning is upon us, we are forced to decide: to make our choices and takes sides immediately. The approaching *eschaton* turns our present crisis into a make-or-break *kairos*.

But that still leaves us with the question of how one is to know that there is an *eschaton* on the horizon. The answer is quite simply that we discover this, as the prophets did, by reading the signs of the times. If one interprets one's own time correctly and especially if one can see the events of one's time with the eyes of God, then one sees clearly to what all the signs are pointing. One can foresee what is going to happen some time in the near future, even if one cannot calculate the exact day or the hour. Prophetic theology begins with some such insight or foresight.

South Africa Today

The Kairos theologians have drawn the conclusion that the present moment in South Africa is a *kairos,* but they have not spelled out very clearly and in a truly prophetic manner why this particular moment should be regarded as a divine *kairos*. Reference is made to the conflict between oppressor and oppressed and to the division in the church that claims the loyalty of both the oppressor and the oppressed. That indeed is a crisis and does indeed raise some serious questions about the meaning of Christianity, but in and by itself does not make our present time a *kairos*.

---

[5]Albert Nolan, *Jesus before Christianity: The Gospel of Liberation* (Cape Town: David Philip, 1976), 77–78.

What is not explicit in the Kairos Document, although it is implied throughout the document, is that what we are now facing is an *eschaton*. What all the signs are now pointing to is that one way or another the day of liberation is near. Apartheid's days are numbered. In the near future this whole oppressive system is going to be utterly destroyed, and a totally new, liberated, and peaceful society will be built up in its place. The people are determined to do this and to do it soon, and all the signs indicate that this drive toward liberation and peace through justice is now unstoppable. Of course, it will be resisted, violently resisted, but it can no longer be stopped, which means that we must expect, unfortunately, more violence, more conflict, and possibly more bloodshed before our society can be turned completely upside down to become a land of justice and peace.

In religious or theological terms, this is our *eschaton*. The day of Yahweh is at hand. The day of reckoning when God will put right what is wrong in our country is now very near. The terrifying seriousness of God's anger and God's love, of God's justice and God's mercy are about to descend upon us in a manner that might well make what the Old Testament prophets were talking about look like child's play. God is no less involved in our present crisis and in the upheaval that is about to take place here than God was in the crisis and in the upheavals of the history of Israel.

That is what makes our present time in South Africa a truly prophetic *kairos*. A time of judgment and salvation. A time for real fear and trembling. A time when everything is at stake. A time for taking a clear stand. A time of tears and sadness that is nevertheless fraught with hope and joyful anticipation. But it is also a time for us to act in the name of God, as the prophets did, to minimize the bloodshed. It is the sort of time when we should drop everything to proclaim from the rooftops that the day of reckoning is upon us and that the day of liberation has dawned. It is a time to appeal for immediate repentance and radical change; a time to call upon all in the world who can still hear the voice of God to do everything in their power, and at whatever cost to themselves, to hasten the downfall of the apartheid regime and so bring the violence of oppression to a speedy end. Now is the time. God is near.

CHAPTER 8

The Spirit of the Prophets

Do not quench the Spirit,
Do not despise prophesying.
(1 Thess. 5:19)

In the Bible, the Holy Spirit is very closely associated with prophecy. The prophets were the people who, more than any others, were moved and motivated by the Spirit. In the Bible, to be moved by the Spirit and to be a prophet is practically the same thing—so much so that in the creed when we want to identify the Spirit we believe in, we say, "We believe in the Holy Spirit who spoke through the prophets."

Before Jesus, this Spirit was given to only a very few people, but at Pentecost the Spirit of God was poured out upon many people and made available to everyone. The immediate result is that everyone can now become like the prophets, can share in the Spirit of the prophets in one way or another. As Peter says in Acts 2:15–21, Joel's prophecy about prophecy has now been fulfilled: "I will pour out upon everyone a portion of my Spirit; your sons and daughters shall prophesy, your young men shall see visions and old men shall dream dreams." "Seeing visions" and "dreaming dreams" are metaphorical ways of referring to the activity of the prophets.

This first appeared in a privately published booklet entitled "Biblical Spirituality," which was a collection of talks given each year during the early 1980s to priests and religious as part of a course entitled Faith and Life.

In the New Testament, prophecy is used in a narrow sense and in a broad general sense. In its narrow sense it applies only to a specific group of Christians who are called prophets (Acts 21:10–11; 1 Cor. 12:28–29), but in its broad general sense it applies to all Christians who are moved by the Spirit no matter what gifts of the Spirit they manifest (Acts 2:17–18; 19:6; Jas. 5:10). In this broad general sense we can say that the spiritual life is always a prophetic life, that in the Bible life in the Spirit is a life lived according to the Spirit of the prophets: "You are the heirs of the prophets" (Acts 3:25).

In other words, if we want to see what a true spiritual life would mean, we would have to begin by taking a careful look at the biblical prophets. There we will see the first great manifestations of the Spirit.

The Greek word *prophetes* has three interrelated meanings: those who speak *out*, those who speak *before*, and those who speak *for*. Prophets speak *out* because they are boldly critical of their world; they speak *before* because they foresee the future; they speak *for* because they speak for God as God's messengers. The rest of this talk corresponds to these three aspects of prophecy.

They Speak Out

The difference between the apostles before Pentecost and after Pentecost is quite clear. Before they received the Holy Spirit they were weak, timid, shy, silent, and unsure of themselves. As soon as they were moved and motivated by the Spirit they became fearless and confident, speaking out boldly and powerfully regardless of the consequences. The Spirit of God enables us to speak out.

This point is made abundantly clear in the lives of the Old Testament prophets. They spoke out against almost everything the Jews of their time were doing, against all the assumptions and accepted norms of behavior. They were characterized by their criticism or speaking out not merely against the enemies of Israel but also against Israel itself, against the leaders of the people, against the priests and the false prophets, against the rich, and against the sacrifices in the Temple. Because of their actions, prophets were usually very unpopular, often persecuted, and even martyred. By New Testament times it was taken for granted that persecution went hand in hand with prophecy (Luke 6:22, 23, 26) and that a prophet was also a martyr (Matt. 23:29, 33).

The Signs of the Times

The prophets' criticism of the status quo was always constructive. They appealed for change or *metanoia* in the light of what they saw, and what they saw were the signs of the times. What made the prophets different from other people were their divinely inspired interpretation of the signs of the times. The message of the prophets is not deduced from eternal principles, nor does it draw eternally valid conclusions. The message of the prophets is time-bound in the sense that it arises out of the signs of a particular time and situation and is addressed to particular people who live in that time and that place. In order to understand the message of a prophet, therefore, one must know the times, the historical situation. The signs of the times vary obviously from time to time. The signs of Jeremiah's time were quite different from the signs of Nahum's time, and the signs that Amos was reading were very different from the signs that Isaiah was interpreting. The apostles and prophets of the New Testament have a whole new set of signs to interpret.

The signs of the times were always historical events, which we today would classify as political, social, economic, cultural, religious, or even psychological events. Many of the prophets were astute political observers who looked into issues like war or the threat of war, the growth and expansion of empires, the value of this or that military alliance, the policy of a king or emperor. While on the home front, they noticed the exploitation of the poor, the lifestyle of the rich, the falsified weights used by traders, and so forth. Then, too, the prophets had amazing insights into the true nature of religious practices like idolatry or the hypocrisy of Temple worship and fasting, and, in New Testament times, religious practices like almsgiving and prayer as well as fasting and the hypocritical legalism of the Pharisees.

All these happenings were seen as signs: good signs and bad signs, signs of what God was doing or planning to do, signs of what God was condemning and rejecting, signs of God's mercy and signs of his anger, signs of hope and signs of impending doom. The point is that God spoke to the prophets in a kind of sign language, except that the signs were the events of their time. The Spirit of God enabled them to read the signs of their times correctly and to speak out about what they saw and foresaw.

They Speak Before

A prophet is essentially a person who looks into the future. But he or she is not a fortune-teller who makes unconditional and absolute predictions about the future. The foretelling or foreseeing of a prophet is always conditional.

The message of every prophet has the same structure. There is an appeal for *metanoia* (repentance, conversion, change) with a warning about the judgment that will follow if the people do not change and a promise of salvation if the people do change. The future judgment or the future salvation are not absolute inevitabilities. They are qualified by conditional clauses: *if* you do not change, *if* you do change. In other words, what the prophet foresees is the consequences of what is being done or not done now. The prophet foresees the future in the present, in present trends, in the signs of the times.

Consequently, if people change now, the future will be different. God relents when humans repent. This principle can be seen explicitly in many parts of the Bible (e.g., Jer. 26:13, 16–23; Jon. 3:10, 4:2; Amos 7:3, 6; Exod. 32:14) and is implicit in all prophecy.

We need to look more closely at this structure or pattern in the prophetic message. Every word spoken by the prophets concerns either judgment, salvation, or *metanoia*.

Judgment

For the prophets, judgment does not refer primarily and immediately to an event in the afterlife. It refers to some future historical event like losing a battle, the fall of Jerusalem, captivity, or exile. In other words, their prophecies of judgment are prophecies of a disaster that will entail terrible suffering for the people. God's judgment is the future punishment for present-day sins. The link between the future and the present in this case is the link between *suffering* and *sin*.

The suffering that follows upon sin is not an arbitrarily imposed punishment; it is what one might call the natural consequences of sin. Sin of its very nature causes harm to those who sin and to others—if not immediately, then at least in the future. All sin has harmful consequences. The warnings of the prophets are not like the threats of a parent who punishes the child for not doing homework by sending him or her to bed without supper. The warnings of the prophets are more like the warnings of the parent who tells the child what harmful consequences not doing one's homework will have in the future—for example, failing exams.

The whole purpose, therefore, of the prophets' warnings about the future is to challenge their contemporaries to change their ways (*metanoia*).

Salvation

Again, salvation for the prophets is not primarily and immediately about eternal salvation or heaven. They foresee a future time of blessing, prosperity, peace, happiness, and justice in the concrete terms of a return from exile or a deliverance (liberation) from war, from domination, from captivity. Here again, this return or deliverance is foreseen as the natural consequence of the justice that is being practiced now or that the people are being challenged to practice now. The only reason that the prophet foretells this is to ensure that people continue in their good works or change their existing evil ways.

There is, however, an important difference between the prophecies of judgment and the prophecies of salvation. In the end there will be salvation. In the end goodness will win over evil. In the end the people will change. That is guaranteed by God. However dismal the present and the immediate future may be, however much judgment and disaster may come, the prophets are always hopeful about the final outcome.

Metanoia

We usually translate *metanoia* as repentance or conversion, but literally it means a change of mind, a change of heart, a change of one's ways and one's behavior. Moreover, this change is always seen as a change from unjust behavior to just behavior. God's demand for change is always a demand for justice.

Metanoia is also a matter of social change rather than individual change. It is a conversion of the whole people or at least the leaders of the people: "Turn back, O Jerusalem." At a later stage in Jeremiah and Ezekiel, and in John the Baptist, the conversion of the individual begins to gain some importance, but even here the change is still for the sake of the nation or at least for the remnant.

The appeal for *metanoia* takes a slightly different form when the people have already changed or are busy changing. In such cases, the prophets have a message of encouragement, consolation, and exhortation—a message of hope. This is particularly evident in that part of Isaiah that is known as the Book of Consolation (chaps. 40–55).

This element of *metanoia* is important because it underlines the prophetic belief that although history is made by God, the

Lord of history, what God will do in the future depends upon what we do now. In other words, we can change history; we can determine the future by our actions.

A Future-Oriented Spirituality

The prophets turned the attention of the people from the past to the future. Instead of trying to understand the present in terms of past events (Exodus, Mount Sinai, King David, etc.), they ask the people to understand the present time in terms of a future act of God. The prophets were forward-looking, future-oriented, and progressive. They wanted the people to change, to plan, to act with a view to the future, and since this future event or *eschaton* would be a qualitatively new event, they appealed to the people to do new things, to make new and unheard-of changes.

Notice how often the prophets use the word "new": the new covenant, a new age, new heart, new spirit, new heaven and new earth, new Jerusalem, or simply that God is going to do a new thing. They challenged the people to break with the past and to look to the newness of God's future: "Remember not the former things. . . . I am going to do a new thing" (Isa. 43:18–19). This is not to say that the prophets wanted the people of Israel to reject all their traditions; they take the traditions and interpret them anew in terms of the new time and the new future. The old covenant is thus used to speak about a future new covenant or new testament; the exodus and the kingdom of the past are used to draw attention to the new exodus and the new kingdom of the future. When the prophets looked back at the events of the past, they saw them as God's promises for the future. Therefore, the past itself points to the future, and in the end we find ourselves facing the future again.

The very last thing that one might say about the prophets would be that they were conservative. They were far ahead of their times and therefore seldom appreciated by their contemporaries. Not that they wanted just any kind of progress. What they looked forward to was the total newness of God's future.

They Speak For

The prophets were very conscious of being God's messengers. They always speak on behalf of God: "Yahweh says." Their message, therefore, was not their own; it was God's message, a revelation from God. Not that God whispered in their ears or sent an angel to dictate a message to them. God spoke to the prophets and revealed Godself to them in the signs of the times.

But how did the prophets read the signs of the times? How were they able to recognize what God was saying to them? This is the really crucial question.

The answer is that the Spirit of God enabled them to feel with God. They were able to share God's attitudes, God's values, God's feelings, God's emotions, which enabled the prophets to see the events of their time as God saw them and to feel the same way about these events as God felt.

The prophets shared God's anger, God's compassion, God's sorrow, God's disappointment, God's revulsion, God's sensitivity for people, and God's seriousness. Nor did they share these things in the abstract; they shared God's feelings about the concrete events of their time. You could say that they had a kind of empathy with God that enabled them to see the world through God's eyes. The Bible does not separate emotions and thoughts. God's word expresses how God feels and thinks. The prophets thought God's thoughts because they shared God's feelings and values. This is what it means to be filled with the Spirit of God, and this is what enables one to read the signs of the times with honesty and truth.

Spiritual writers today would call this "mystical union with God." But before I elaborate on that, let us look more carefully and in greater detail at how the prophets experienced this empathy with God. We confine ourselves in this discussion to the prophet Jeremiah and look first at a few texts that give expression to God's feelings and sentiments, then a few texts in which Jeremiah shares God's feelings about the events of his time, and finally some texts in which Jeremiah's feelings clash with the feelings of God. Here at last we will be looking at the core of Jeremiah's spiritual life, his prayer, and his struggle to achieve union with God.

a. There are many expressions of God's anger, but a look at 5:7–11 will suffice. In 2:1–13 we see God's disappointment and dismay, and in 14:17–18 God's sadness. Then again in 30:10–11 we have an example of God's tremendous compassion for his people.

b. In 23:9, when Jeremiah feels overwhelmed by God's words, we should remember that a word is not just a thought but an expression of feeling. Jeremiah felt the anger of God, in particular, filling his whole being. He tells us about this in 6:10–11 and 15:17.

c. In those passages that we call the Prayers or Confessions of Jeremiah, we find the prophet complaining to God and clashing with God either because Jeremiah cannot share God's anger and pleads for gentleness (10:23–25) or because Jeremiah's selfish anger is not shared by God (11:20; 12:1–6; 18:19–23). This becomes a crisis for Jeremiah. He wishes he had never been born, and he wants to give up being a prophet (15:10–21; 20:7–18).

Jeremiah sometimes found it difficult to understand what God was doing and why. But he does not just accept this in blind faith. He questions God. He complains and meditates on the problem in a spirit of critical reflection. He felt that he had to question in order to try to understand. If he had not done this, he would have had very little insight into the signs of his times; he would never have come to that union with God that enabled him to see what God saw in the events of his time.

Jeremiah did, of course, experience moments of peace (31:26), but this was a hard-won peace after much struggle and real agony of mind. We tend to think that we have prayed well only when we have experienced peace and that union with God is always a calm, peaceful, and unemotional experience. This is not so, because sometimes God is not peaceful and calm. Sometimes God is very, very upset and angry.

God's Anger

Today we tend to find God's anger an embarrassment. The prophetic expression of God's raging anger tends to fill us with dismay. But, in fact, until we can share something of this divine feeling, our spiritual life will remain immature and our union with God will be abstract and unreal.

God's compassion is always accompanied by anger and indignation. They are two sides of the same coin, because one cannot really love and have real compassion if one is not able to get angry and indignant. When one person harms another, when some people are cruel to others, when they exploit them and oppress them, then real compassion for those who are being harmed and oppressed necessarily entails anger and indignation toward those who make them suffer.

This is not the anger of hatred or selfishness; it is the anger of compassion. God is angry with them for their sake. It is the anger that challenges them to change by making clear the *seriousness* of what they are doing. In the Temple courtyard Jesus felt compassion for the poor who were exploited by the traders and money changers. His anger made it quite clear how terribly serious this sin of exploitation was.

We should be careful not to trivialize God. God is very serious about the cruelty of one person to another in the world today. Unless we can share God's seriousness we will always remain far from God, and any experience of apparent closeness to God would be an illusion.

Sharing God's anger can be a liberating experience and a source of drive, energy, and determination in our spiritual lives. We all have an aggressive instinct. We can use it in a selfish way against our neighbor, or we can turn it in upon ourselves or bottle it up. Or we can use it as a source of drive and determination to fight sin and suffering in the world. This is what the saints did, which is why they were such determined people and why they had such a healthy sense of indignation about the sinfulness of the world.

Today

Any new spirituality today, and especially a biblical spirituality, would have to include a very serious attempt to read the signs of our times. We cannot do this alone. We must try to do it together. But most of all we must not avoid it because then we will quench the spirit and destroy any possibility of a genuine spiritual life. Jesus himself tells us to read the signs of the times (Luke 12:54–57), and the Second Vatican Council reminds us of the urgent need to do this today (see the opening chapters of *Gaudium et Spes*).

Moreover, a healthy spiritual life will include a constant conversion or willingness to change and a tendency to look to the newness of the future rather than a harking back to the past. Hankering after the past is not an attitude that comes from the Holy Spirit. We must be willing to sacrifice the security that we get from reliance upon the values and practices of the past.

A life in the Spirit is a life of speaking out about what is wrong in our world, our society, our church, and our community; of speaking out about the future we are heading for or should be heading for; of speaking out about how God must feel about the events of our time. This at least is the direction in which we must move if we are to be faithful to the Spirit of the prophets, who is the Spirit of God.

At the heart of all of this is our personal struggle with God in prayer. We need to become totally honest before God about our real feelings and attitudes concerning the events of our time, and we need to be totally honest about why we feel that way and about whether God feels the same way as we do about these events. Do we really share God's love and compassion for the poor and the oppressed, and do we really share God's anger and indignation? Do we make God according to our own image and likeness, or do we allow God to remake us according to God's image and likeness?

PART 4

Hoping for a Better World

Many people hope and believe that another world, a better world, is possible. But as Christians, what is the content of that hope? What kind of a better world should we hope for? For Nolan, as Christians, we should hope for a world that is driven by God's will. The better world that we should hope for is a world in which God's will is done. Hence, in the prayer of Our Father, we say, "Thy will be done." God's will is that which is good for everyone. "What God wants is whatever is best for all of us together, not what is best for some at the expense of others." We sometimes call this the "common good."

In the chapters that follow, Nolan outlines the gospel values that form the reality of the common good. Jesus exemplified these values: the values of sharing, solidarity, justice, dignity, and service, among others. He goes on to describe how religious life should become a prophetic witness to these gospel values.

CHAPTER 9

Gospel Values

The great leap forward from the Old Testament to the New Testament can be described as a leap from the external observance of laws to the internalization of values, from the letter of the law to the freedom of the Spirit. At some stage in our spiritual lives we will have to make a similar leap forward to freedom.

Jesus challenges us to transcend all laws, rules, and principles, even the Ten Commandments, in order to take full responsibility for our actions. Jesus challenges us to be free and to judge for ourselves what is right and what is wrong. The ability to decide for ourselves when it would be appropriate to keep a law or a rule and when it would not be appropriate requires a great deal of personal freedom and responsibility. Many people find this kind of freedom quite frightening. They prefer to be told what to do, or they prefer to have absolutely binding laws and rules so that they don't have to take the responsibility of deciding for themselves. This is a very serious obstacle to progress in the spiritual life that quenches the Spirit of freedom.

However, the gospel does provide us with guidelines. It gives us Jesus himself as a model of true freedom, and it makes clear the values by which he lived. We can experience the freedom of the Spirit by learning to internalize these values and to live by them ourselves.

This is taken from the booklet "Biblical Spirituality" published privately in 1986 (see chap. 8 above).

Basically there is only one value in the gospel: the value of love or compassion—justice of the heart. Or you could put it another way and say that the one and only value in the gospel is people. People are more important than things, more important than laws, more important than money or status or knowledge or power or anything else in the world. God has one great value: people. That is why we speak about love, compassion, justice. These things stress the all-importance of people.

However, in order to understand the practical implications of this one great value, we need to subdivide it into several different values relating to different areas of life or to the different forms of lovelessness and injustice that have to be overcome. In the gospel we find four dominant values. They are simply four ways of loving or practicing justice, and they correspond to (and are opposed to) the four dominant worldly values of the society in which Jesus lived.

Jesus lived in a Jewish society, but the dominant values of that society were not the values of the Old Testament any more than the values of our society are the values of the New Testament. The values of Jesus' society, like ours, were very much worldly values: money, power, status, group selfishness. Jesus responded to each of these dominant worldly values by presenting the corresponding godly value. So if we divide the one great value of love into four, it is in response to the four dominant values of the world.

We now address these values one by one. We first define the area of concern and then the worldly value and the corresponding gospel value in that area.

Sharing

The area of life we are concerned with here covers everything to do with money and possessions. It includes what we today call our standard of living: the kind of house we live in, the type of food we eat, the clothing we wear, and all the other material goods we use. It also includes the buying and selling of goods and the way these goods are produced, manufactured, and consumed. The Spirit of Jesus must motivate us in this large area of life as much as anywhere else in life.

A very high percentage of the sayings and parables in the four Gospels, especially in Luke, are about money and possessions. This is not accidental. Money and possessions held an important place in the thinking of Jesus' contemporaries. The Pharisees are described as lovers of money (Luke 16:14), and most people, rich and poor, considered the possession of great wealth a blessing from God. In other words, the worldly value here that people were striving for was to be rich, to have a high standard of living.

Against this value Jesus took an uncompromising stand: you cannot serve both God and money (Matt. 6:24). You must choose one or the other. You cannot have it both ways. Those who choose money exclude God, in fact, even if they imagine that they have not done so. Those who choose money exclude themselves from the kingdom. They are like camels imagining that they can get through the eye of a needle (Mark 10:25).

Jesus calls those who choose money instead of God "the rich." He does not say "those rich people who are attached to their money" or "those who became rich by exploiting others." He simply condemns anyone who is rich for as long as they remain rich. "Woe to you who are rich" (Luke 6:24). The only possible qualification to this in the Gospels is the qualification implicit in the parable of Lazarus and the Rich Man (Luke 16:19–31). The rich man is condemned to hell for one simple reason: he was rich and remained rich while there was a beggar on his doorstep—that is, while other people were destitute and hungry.

What, then, must the rich do? They must simply cease to be rich. They must undergo a very basic conversion. They must turn from money to God. They must become detached from their wealth and then prove this in practice by giving it away, by sharing it with those who are in need. Jesus puts it very simply and straightforwardly. His advice to the rich is simply, "Sell your possessions and share the proceeds with the poor" (Matt. 6:19–21; Luke 12:33–34; 14:33). There has been a tendency to apply this only to religious who take a vow of poverty. But in the Gospels Jesus applies it to everyone who wants to be his disciple, everyone who wants to follow him (and, of course, has possessions to sell). He says this quite explicitly in Luke 14:33: "None of you can be my disciple unless he gives up all his possessions."

In the time of Jesus and in the early church, this was one of the most important conditions for becoming a Christian, it was part of the cost of discipleship (Luke 14:28–33). We see Zacchaeus giving up everything except what he really needs (Luke 19:8). We see the first Christians selling land and houses and sharing the proceeds (Acts 2:44–46; 4:34; 5:11).

The gospel value here is *sharing*, the purpose of which is not simply to prove one's detachment from material things; the purpose of this sharing is to ensure that the poor are fed, that everyone may have what he or she needs, or that nobody may suffer because they are in need. In other words sharing is simply love, compassion, and justice lived out in the area of money and possessions. If you remain indifferent to the needs of the poor and the needy and refuse to share with them what you have, you have not even begun to love your neighbor or to practice justice, and you certainly cannot claim to be compassionate.

Nothing in the Gospels has been so consistently and unashamedly watered down as Jesus' teaching about money and sharing. The worldly value of money and a high standard of living has completely overshadowed the gospel value of sharing. Most Christians try to have it both ways: God and money. But what this means in practice, as Jesus says, is that they worship money, or what they call their standard of living, instead of God, because "you cannot serve two masters."

Money presents a very serious obstacle to progress in the spiritual life. So many of us are enslaved to our possessions, our material comforts, our so-called standard of living. We are often willing to sacrifice other things, like our time and energy, but our standard of living is sacred. Yet one of the most liberating experiences in the spiritual life is the experience of becoming liberated from our possessiveness, becoming really detached from material things and sharing with those who are in need.

This is not just a matter of charity to beggars at the door. It is a matter of politics and economics, of capitalist exploitation, of structures that enable the rich to get richer while the poor become poorer; it is a matter of totally unequal standards of living. The life of the Spirit is about the quality of our living rather than the material standard of our living. Solidarity with the poor is central to all biblical spirituality.

Human Dignity

The second area of life to be looked at is that of *social relationships*. We are concerned here with the way in which people relate to one another in society; the basis upon which they accord one another dignity, respect, honor, and prestige; and the values that determine these relationships.

In Jesus' society, people were treated with various degrees of honor and dignity or given hardly any respect or no respect at all, according to their status or position in the society. What people valued most was their status, and the most important fact about any other person was his or her position on the social ladder. This false, worldly value determined all social relationships: how you addressed another person, the tone of voice you used, where you sat at banquets and in the synagogue, the type of clothing you wore, with whom you mixed, and whom you invited to a meal.

Jesus contradicted this worldly value in no uncertain terms. He castigated the Pharisees in particular for their status seeking. He condemned status symbols like special kinds of dress (Matt. 23:5), places of honor (Matt. 23:6), and special titles and forms of greeting (Matt. 23:7), but most of all he rejected any use of religious practices to boost one's standing in the society (Matt. 6:1–18).

Jesus even finds it necessary to correct his own disciples again and again for their own status seeking. They keep arguing about who among them is the greatest (Matt. 18:1; Mark 9:33–34), and they compete with one another for the places of honor on his right and his left (Mark 10:35–37).

What Jesus demands then is that we give up all concern for status and prestige. We must be content with the last place, the bottom rung of the ladder—not because we especially want the last place, but because our place in society is no longer a value for us. Jesus demonstrated this very clearly in his own life. He treated everyone with equal respect and honor. He mixed with the outcasts of the society: beggars, cripples, prostitutes, and tax collectors. He blessed the poor and all who were despised and abused by society (Luke 6:20–23). Children are treated with the same respect as adults, and women are given the same status as men. Jesus was well known for ignoring the status and rank that society accorded a person (Mark 12:14), and he himself lost status completely. His society accused him of being a drunkard, a glutton, a sinner, and a blasphemer (Matt. 11:19; 26:65), and eventually they executed him as a common criminal.

The opposite value here, the gospel value, is *human dignity*. Equal dignity, respect, and honor must be given to all human beings because they are all made in the image and likeness of God. In the eyes of God we are all equal in status, dignity, and value. The social ladder of every and any society (including the church) must be rejected as worldly, ungodly, and sinful.

The internalization of this gospel value is very important for our spiritual lives. In the first place, it is the basis of all genuine *humility*. If we model ourselves upon the society in which we live and base our self-respect upon our status, rank, class, race, nationality, education, intelligence, or even virtue, our self-respect becomes pride. If we go to the opposite extreme and try to have no self-respect at all, we are guilty of a false humility or self-abasement that is an insult to the God who made us in God's own image and likeness. However, once we base our self-respect upon our God-given dignity as human beings, recognizing that we share this dignity with all other human beings, we have a genuine and liberating humility. All the burdensome worries about achieving dignity and worth through education, promotion, prestige, and success are removed from our shoulders. We are free to be ourselves. We have become true and genuine.

Second, respect for human dignity is the basis of *love* and *justice* in social relationships. To love everyone in our society is to treat them all with equal respect. To practice justice is to put right the wrongs of discrimination, prejudice, and privilege and to work for real equality, real brotherhood/sisterhood in the church and in society. The spirit of Jesus urges us on to strive in every way possible for equality and justice.

This is easier said than done. Inequality permeates not only the structures of our society and our church but also the very structures of our thinking. Until we can rid ourselves of this concern for status, we will not be on the same wavelength as Jesus.

Human Solidarity

The third area of life is that of *social groupings*, and our concern is with the phenomenon of group selfishness. The human race is divided into social groups like nations, tribes, clans, families, cultures, classes, races, religions, and church denominations. These social conformations give us a sense of belonging, and often enough we develop strong feelings of loyalty and group solidarity.

In Jesus' society, social groups were all-important. People experienced such a strong feeling of solidarity with the other members of their group that it would be possible to say to someone from outside of the group, "Whatever you do to the least of my kinsmen and women, you do to me."

The problem here is not the fact of social groups, nor even their solidarity. The problem is the selfishness of the group vis-à-vis other groups. We tend to think of selfishness only in terms of individuals, but in the time of Jesus—and indeed in our time, too—group selfishness was something far more serious, dangerous, and harmful. The sinful, worldly value here is the selfishness and exclusiveness of group solidarity.

Jesus contradicted this social value. He reached out beyond his own social, cultural, and religious group to embrace the whole human race as his brothers and sisters, as his kinsmen and kinswomen, as his neighbors. The Old Testament commandment to love one's neighbor had always been interpreted to mean that one should live in solidarity with those who are close to one, the members of one's social group (see Lev. 19:16–18). This eventually led to the extrabiblical saying, "Love your neighbor and hate your enemy." Jesus contradicts this with his well-known command, "Love your enemies." Your neighbor is every other human being, including those outside of your group, including even those who are your enemies, those who hate you and curse you (Luke 6:27–35). In other words, the value for Jesus is not group solidarity but *human solidarity*.

To treat solidarity with the human race as a value does not mean that we no longer value loyalty to and solidarity with our social group. It means that human solidarity becomes more important to us than any group solidarity. The only way to ensure that none of our group loyalties ever becomes selfish and sinful is to subordinate them to the more basic value of solidarity with the human race.

This can be an amazingly liberating experience and a very profound discovery of one's true identity. It enables me to transcend the limitations of the various social groupings that categorize and define me. Who I am? a Christian? a Catholic?

a Dominican? a priest? a South African? No. In the very first place I am a member of the human race, made in the image and likeness of God. My first loyalty is to the human family. Everything else is secondary.

Paradoxically this basic loyalty to the human race makes me a Christian, a follower of Jesus Christ who identified himself with all human beings: "Whatever you do to the least of my brothers and sisters you do to me." To discover Christ or God in another human being is to transcend all the other things I might have in common with that person and to experience very simply and profoundly the humanity we have in common. This is Christian love, this is divine compassion, this is what moved the Samaritan in the parable to do what he did for a socially despised Jew. We are all brothers and sisters, and God is our Father.

Service

Our fourth area of concern is that of *power*. Most of us have some measure of power and authority, some kind of responsibility for some other people. Power is not only a factor in politics and in society; it is also a factor in the church, in convents, in parishes, in families, in associations. In almost every corner of life we find people jostling for power, using it and abusing it, dominating others and trying to control them.

Power in itself is not a false, worldly value. The false value is the worldly way of exercising power and authority, the use of power and authority to *dominate* and *oppress* others.

In Jesus' society this is how power and authority were generally used. He contradicts it as a pagan value that must be replaced by the gospel value of using all power and authority to serve others:

You know that among the pagans their so-called rulers lord it over them, and their great men make their authority felt. This is not to happen among you. No; anyone who wants to become great among you must be your servant, and anyone who wants to be first among you must be slave to all. For the son of man himself did not come to be served but to serve and to give his life as a ransom for many. (Mark 1:42–45)

There is no mistaking the two different ways in which power and authority can be exercised. It is the difference between domination and service, between wanting to be served and wanting to serve, between using power as an oppressor and using power as a liberator. No genuine spiritual life is possible without an appreciation of the difference between these two values, these two spirits: the spirit of domination and oppression and the spirit of service and liberation.

We know that the Spirit of God is moving in us when we give up dominating others in any way at all and when we no longer feel the need to assert ourselves by controlling everything they do. The liberating experience of transcending our selfishness includes the experience of serving people because we love them rather than because we want recognition, thanks, and admiration from them. We know that the Spirit of God is moving in the church when church structures become more and more structures of real service and ministry, rather than structures of domination and control. We know that the Spirit of God is moving in our society when we see that political structures cease to be structures of oppression and slavery and begin to be used to serve the needs of all the people.

~

These are God's values. They are the values implicit in God's passion for justice and his love for the human race. They are the values that govern God's feelings and emotions. They are the values of the Spirit as revealed in Jesus Christ.

These values must transform our spiritual lives and especially our struggle with God in prayer. They are the values that we must spread in every form of apostolate, ministry, or evangelization so that they may gradually transform and liberate the whole world. In our reading of the signs of the times, these values enable us to recognize the signs of hope, the seeds of the kingdom in our world today.

CHAPTER 10

Consecrated Life as a Prophetic Witness

Consecrated life is not only a way of life that gives witness to the reality of God, the relevance of Jesus, and the work of the Spirit, it is also a way of life that contradicts the values of the world, the values of most of our society. It is a prophetic witness because it speaks out like all the prophets when others remain silent. Consecrated life is prophetic because it dares to stand up against the worldly values that most people just take for granted. It is prophetic because it wants to transcend the culture of sex, the culture of money, and the culture of individualism. The witness of religious life is that another world is possible. There is an alternative. We have adopted this consecrated way of life in order to remind people that a world of love and justice and peace and happiness is possible. We call it the kingdom or reign of God.

This prophetic way of life finds expression in the three vows or promises of our consecration: poverty, chastity, and obedience.

The Vow of Poverty

The greatest scandal in the world today is that there is so much poverty, hunger, and destitution in an ocean of excessive wealth and plenty, in a time when there is an oversupply of

This was the second of two talks given at a meeting of South Africa's LCCL (Leadership Conference of Consecrated Life) in April 2007.

food and resources. This is the great injustice of our times: the economic injustice of greed, gluttony, exploitation, and theft. What could be more selfish and sinful than the growing number of people who hoard more money and possessions than they can ever spend while others are starving? This scandalous situation is justified by appealing to the right to private property. "It's mine. I earned it or inherited it. It is all legal. I have a perfect right to accumulate as much as I like, no matter how many children are dying of hunger." That is not only immoral; it is positively obscene. In fact, it is idolatry. Our society for the most part worships Mammon. Our culture is becoming more and more a culture of money. The only value many people appreciate is the value of money. Everything today has a price tag.

In this social and economic context we consecrate ourselves to God by voluntarily giving up our right to private ownership. We take a vow of poverty. Calling it a vow of poverty, however, is somewhat misleading. We are not solemnly promising God that we will be poor, needy, and destitute. We want our lives to be a prophetic witness against the scandal of poverty and destitution. How do we do this? By promising to share with others in community.

The vow we take is a commitment to sharing rather than to poverty. We give up our right to ownership in order to own all things in common with our fellow religious in community. The result for those who share and hold everything in common is that nobody will be in need, nobody will be destitute. This is precisely what happened in the first sharing community of Christians in Jerusalem. We are told in the book of Acts that because they held everything in common, "There was not a needy person among them" (5:34).

Our vow is not to become needy but to share so that we will not be needy. Perhaps we should change the name of the vow from a vow of poverty to a vow of sharing, a solemn commitment to voluntarily give up our right to private ownership in favor of a life of common ownership.

While the sharing we are talking about here is primarily the sharing within a religious community, our spirit of sharing should extend beyond the community to others who are in need. A rich sharing community that does not want to share with the poor would be guilty of group selfishness. This is where a simple lifestyle comes in. We do not want to be needy and destitute ourselves, but we also do not want to have more than we need.

If we did this and lived it fully and manifestly, it would become a powerful prophetic witness against the greed, selfishness, and injustice of the rich; it would be a witness in favor of the poor, the destitute, and the starving, and it would be a prophetic sign of the kind of world we hope for in the future—a world in which the resources of the earth are shared among all. This is what Jesus stood for. He taught us to be willing to share with one another because we love one another. The kingdom we look forward to will be a kingdom of sharing.

The Vow of Chastity

The vow of chastity is not just a solemn promise to abstain from sex. That is the negative side of the vow, but it also has a positive side. Positively it is a solemn promise to love everyone, to pursue a kind of love that includes all human beings. The vow is a special kind of commitment to universal, unconditional, and inclusive love. Explicit sexual relationships are excluded only because we want to reach out to the unloved and the lonely, the rejected and the marginalized, the blind, the lame, and the crippled, to prostitutes and sexually exploited women and children—to everyone. As Joan Chittister says so eloquently, "Chastity is not about not loving. It is about learning to love well, to love grandly, to love with sweeping gestures."

Unfortunately, many of us who take the vow do become somewhat cold and loveless. We seem to buy into our society's assumption that love is sex, that making love is a synonym for sexual intercourse, and that if there is no sex there is no love and no intimacy—so those who do not have sexual relationships are necessarily without passion and warmth. But our vow is meant to contradict precisely this understanding of love. Our vow is supposed to give witness to the passion and faithfulness of divine love, the love for everyone about which Jesus was speaking. To quote Joan Chittister again, "The passionate religious falls in love with soup kitchen people, and dirty kids, and grieving widows and dying AIDS patients. . . . [Moreover] the religious loves without binding people to herself or himself. . . . The effects can be astounding."

For those who have never been loved and who feel that they are unlovable, and for those who have been loved for their bodies or other qualities and never just for themselves, the unconditional love poured out upon them by a vowed religious is of inestimable value.

In South Africa today, whether we are black or white, traditional or modern, religious or not, we live in a cultural context that worships and idolizes sex. I do not wish to imply that anything is wrong with sex in itself. Sex is a wonderful part of God's creation, but our society does seem to have rendered it out of perspective. We have developed a culture that is obsessed with sex. What our society needs is not more sex but more love, more selfless care and concern for one another.

The problem is not sex but selfishness, the loveless abuse or misuse of sex. The problem is the exploitation of women and men and children when they are treated as sex objects instead of persons. The problem is rape and child abuse and pornography.

In this context our vow provides a prophetic witness to another possible world: a world of unconditional, universal, and inclusive love.

Perhaps we should consider changing the name of this vow, too—from a vow of *chastity* to a vow of *love*, a solemn commitment to a way of life that will enable us to pour out our love upon everyone as a prophetic act of witness.

The Vow of Obedience

I have spoken about our modern secular culture as a culture of money and of sex. This culture worships money and idolizes sex. But it has one other characteristic. It is also a culture of selfish individualism. What we see all around us is the cult of the individual: me, me, me, my career, my fulfillment, my interests, my will, my needs, my happiness, and doing it my way.

The cultural ideal of the Western industrialized world is the self-made, self-sufficient, autonomous individual who stands alone, not needing anyone else. Freedom and happiness are equated with independence and self-sufficiency. This is the context in which we take a vow of obedience to our religious community.

The vow of obedience contradicts the worldly value of selfish individualism. It is a commitment to the common good, what is best for everyone. We sacrifice our own will, our own interests, our own career for the sake of the common good. We commit ourselves to the needs of others.

Here again maybe it would be a good idea to change the name of the vow from a vow of *obedience* to a vow to pursue *the common good* within a religious community.

Obedience has unfortunately come to be associated with a slavish submission to the will of others. It has often come to mean acting like a robot or a dog that has been trained to just obey. The vow of obedience has too often kept some religious childish and immature.

But it does not have to be misunderstood in this way. It can become a powerful prophetic witness against selfish individualism and in favor of the common good. In this way, our vow can become another sign of the future world we believe in and hope for, a world in which we will all work for the common good of the whole human race and of all God's creation.

If there is something our world needs more than anything else, it is men and women who will not only preach the good news, but who will embody Jesus' message in a consecrated way of life that acts as a prophetic witness to the values of the future.

People of Hope

There is a very important sense in which religious men and women can provide leadership in South Africa today: not by occupying positions of power in the church or in government, but by *standing out in our society as people of hope*. We have seen how our consecrated way of life, our vows could be seen as a prophetic witness against the values of the world and as a witness to another possible world; our vows could be seen as signs of hope for a better world for everyone.

But that, of course, is not at all how most people see us. In fact, we seldom see ourselves like that. Often enough we feel as hopeless and helpless as anyone else in the face of all the problems we encounter in South Africa today. So how do we become people of hope ourselves and signs of hope for others?

What is the basis of our hope? Many South Africans are hopeful about our country and its future. But there are others, and they are the ones who feature prominently in the media, who see only the problems and who despair that we will ever get it right. More and more people, including Christians, are giving up hope about anything in today's world, in South Africa or elsewhere. They say they see no signs at all of hope—or very few signs. But as Christians, as true followers of Jesus, we should not be basing our hope on signs—any kind of signs or any number of signs. The basis of our hope is God and God alone. Even if we were living in a time and place with no signs of hope at all, we would still be filled with hope because we have put all our hope and trust in God—or at least we try to do so. In the words of Paul, "We hope against hope."

The Culture of Blame

What we have to transcend in South Africa is not just the pessimism of so many people but also the culture of blame that has developed over the years. We live in what I call a culture of blame. Whenever anything goes wrong, we tend to look around for someone to blame. We point fingers and impute guilt. We feel restless and dissatisfied until we can find someone to accuse. Finding someone to blame gives us a feeling of satisfaction.

Almost everybody indulges in this culture of blame or at least is tempted to do so: politicians, journalists, editors, commentators, academics, and, saddest of all, the church. But Jesus didn't do it. He didn't go around pointing fingers at people. He didn't go around hammering sinners. He saw them as people in need of healing, forgiveness, and love. He saw them as hurt, wounded, or lost. When we look around for someone to blame, we are unable to obtain an unbiased view of the world, and we are unable to see the finger of God at work in our world.

Our consecrated life can become a prophetic witness against this culture of blame and a witness to the hopefulness that comes from putting all one's trust in God. This happens when we are seen as people who have made God the basis of their hope for the future of South Africa and the world.

Taking vows of poverty, chastity, and obedience can be seen as a grand gesture of hope in the future. Remember the prophet Jeremiah's grand gesture of hope at the very moment that Jerusalem was under siege and about to fall to the Chaldeans. The people were devastated. They had lost all hope for the future. But in the midst of all this despair, Jeremiah bought a field because he believed that there was hope for the future. He had put all his trust in God. His gesture was a sign that he hoped against hope because of his faith in God (Jer. 32:24–25, 42–43).

However, our vows would not be seen as gestures of hope for the future if we ourselves in all we do or say are quite obviously not hopeful and not confident about the future. We have to be seen and experienced as people who hope against hope, who remain hopeful in all circumstances.

Our hope can become itself a sign of hope that strengthens others and witnesses to the value of putting all one's trust in God. When we act hopefully and when we speak with hope and confidence, we encourage others to act boldly and confidently, and enable them not to give up hope.

When called upon to do so, we should be prepared to give an account of our hope as Peter says in his First Letter (1 Pet. 3:15). We give an account of our hope by telling people that we put all our hope and trust in God. But we also give an account of our hope by pointing to what we see as the signs of God's work in our country, in the world, and in the church today.

The International Congress

One of the truly great signs of hope for the future of the church has been the 2004 International Congress on Consecrated Life. Some of you will have heard about it. In fact, some of you may have been there, but for those who do not know about it, let me explain that it was the first congress of its kind. It was the first time that the leadership of different religious institutes and of national conferences, like our South African LCCL, had come together to reflect upon the present and the future of our consecrated life.

Together the congress analyzed the significance, effectiveness, and relevance of religious life in today's postmodern world. They celebrated and gave thanks to God for the timeless gift of religious life. They discovered, welcomed, and reinforced emerging new forms of consecrated living. Sharing their experiences of consecrated living, the 850 participants from the four corners of the globe discovered their common passion for Jesus Christ and for all human beings, especially the most vulnerable. The theme of the congress was "Passion for Christ, Passion for Humanity."

This congress was an immense sign of hope, not only for the future of religious life, but also for the future of the church as a whole. Religious life is what one may call the prophetic arm of the church. What seems to have been happening at this congress was that the prophetic voice of the church was being consolidated. Religious together have rediscovered the importance of their prophetic witness in the church and in the world.

CHAPTER 11

Who Is My Neighbor?

Who is my neighbor? The question has echoed down through the ages from one generation of Christians to another. It is all very well to say that the Great Commandment is to love God and to love one's neighbor, but who is my neighbor?

For Jesus our neighbor is everyone—absolutely everyone without exception. No matter who they are or what they have ever said or done.

We know that. And yet down through the ages we have made exceptions. We have excluded these people or those people. *Not them!* We have excluded people who are different from us, people of a different race or religion or nationality or political camp.

In Jesus' time the Jews excluded Samaritans. They hated Samaritans because Samaritans were heretics and traitors. They were not pure Jews. They lived in a neighboring country but they were not thought of as neighbors, as brothers and sisters.

So, when this good Jewish lawyer who had kept all the commandments (he says) asks Jesus the big question, "But who is my neighbor?" Jesus answers by telling him a story about a Samaritan who went out of his way to help a Jew who had fallen among thieves.

This was a sermon preached on March 21, 2008, during an ecumenical service preceding the annual Good Friday procession through the streets of Durban.

Is he not also your neighbor? Are Samaritans not also our neighbors? Should we not love them, too? In fact, despite the hostility between Jews and Samaritans, this Samaritan showed amazing love for a Jew.

Jesus then challenges this Jewish lawyer powerfully by saying, "Now why don't you go and do the same yourself? You can learn something from that Samaritan."

The lawyer would have found that very difficult to accept. I can hear him saying, "But how can we love these people? They are our enemies; just as the Romans are our enemies. Are we supposed to love the merciless and cruel Romans, too?"

Jesus' answer was shocking, to say the least. "You have been taught to love your neighbor and to hate your enemy. But I say to you, *love your enemies.*"

In other words, all your worst and most wicked enemies are also your neighbors. Love them, too.

Jesus then spells out what this means:

> "Do good to those who hate you.
> Bless those who curse you.
> Pray for those who persecute you."

This is what Jesus himself did, and this is what made him such a great person—such a magnificent example of unconditional love. He identified with all human beings, and so he was able to say, "Whatever you do to the least of these my brothers and sisters, you do to me. And whatever you did not do for the least of these my brothers and sisters, you did not do for me."

As we sit here on this Good Friday morning in Durban in the year 2008, we are faced once again with the question, "Who is my neighbor?"

And the answer is *Jesus*—hanging there in agony on the cross. He is my neighbor. He represents all human beings. He has identified himself with all of them. Whatever you do to the least of my brothers and sisters you do to me? If you don't love them, you don't love me. If you treated the hungry and the thirsty as your neighbors and fed them and gave them something to drink, you did it to me. If you clothed the naked and visited the sick, you did it to me. On the other hand, if you refused to help them, you refused to help me.

If you refuse to treat people of a different race or religion or nationality as your neighbor, as your brother or sister, then you are refusing to treat me as your brother, says Jesus.

We know the story of Paul's great conversion on the road to Damascus. He was struck off his horse by a great light, and he heard a voice saying. "Saul, Saul, why do you persecute me?"

"Who are you?" asks Paul.

"I am Jesus, whom you are persecuting," came the answer. Paul was persecuting the early Christians because he saw them as his enemies. But Jesus says, "You are persecuting *me.*"

As we sit here today contemplating Jesus on the cross, we ask ourselves, "Who are we persecuting? Who are we excluding? Who are we not treating as a brother or a sister? And who is *my* neighbor?"

Some South Africans find it difficult to accept our neighbors from across our borders. We call it xenophobia, the fear and even hatred of foreigners. We persecute them, don't we? Perhaps today we can hear Jesus saying, "When you do that, you are persecuting me."

We think particularly of the millions of people in Zimbabwe, our neighboring country, who are suffering and will continue to suffer. They are our brothers and sisters. We dare not exclude them from our love and concern, lest we be accused of excluding Jesus himself. "Whatever you do to them, you do to me."

This year, Good Friday falls on March 21—Human Rights Day.

The question "Who is my neighbor?" can also be asked in terms of human rights. We can ask, "Who has the right to life? Who has the right to freedom of association, freedom of expression, and freedom of religion? Who has the right to housing, food, water, and health care? Are some people to be excluded?"

No. These human rights enshrined in our Constitution are for everyone, for all our people. To exclude some people is to exclude Jesus.

March 21 was formerly known as Sharpeville Day. We remember that fateful day when sixty-nine people were shot dead and many more were injured—a gross violation of human rights if there ever was one. A massacre.

Some of us can remember the pictures in the newspapers at that time, pictures of bodies spread out across the streets of Sharpeville. Today we can look at that scene and say, "There are my neighbors—every one of them."

And then we can look at those who did the shooting and say, "They, too, are my neighbors." We can and must deplore what they did. We must hate their sin and reject it in no uncertain terms. But what Jesus is challenging us to do is to hate the sin but love the sinner—as he did.

The crucifixion of Jesus Christ that we commemorate on Good Friday was surely the greatest violation of human rights ever perpetrated. Jesus was the victim of an unspeakable crime, but as he was dying he managed to pray for those who persecuted him. "Father forgive them," he prayed, "for they know not what they do."

My neighbor is everyone, all human beings—without exception.

CHAPTER 12

Jesus and the Oikos Journey

I would like to make a contribution to Diakonia's Oikos Journey by suggesting a theological reflection that relates Jesus and his spirituality to South Africa's economic crisis. What would Jesus say about poverty and wealth in South Africa today.

The Worship of Mammon

Jesus condemned the economic system of his time in no uncertain terms. He called it idolatry—the worship of Mammon. We remember his famous challenge to the people of his time:

> "You cannot serve two masters
> You cannot serve both God and money
> You will have to choose one or the other."

In a way it is as simple as that. Take your pick. Make your choice. However, in practice it is not as simple as that. It is, in fact, very difficult to make a clear choice. People can be related to Mammon in three ways.

First, there are the people who have made a clear choice for money. Money is their God. They will do absolutely anything to protect their money and possessions and to acquire more.

This comes from a talk given at a Diakonia Luncheon in Durban on December 4, 2006. The *Oikos Journey* was a theological reflection on the economic crisis in South Africa published by the Diakonia Council of Churches in 2006.

Such people are slaves. They are no longer free, if they ever were. Money has become their master. They are chained to this master, to Mammon.

Second, there are those who try to compromise. They imagine that they can serve both God and money at the same time, but that is an illusion. We need to try to disillusion them and challenge them as Jesus did.

This is beautifully illustrated in the story of Jesus' encounter with the rich young man as told in Matthew, Mark, and Luke. The rich young man in this story is the perfect example of someone who is trying to serve two masters: God and Mammon. He tells Jesus that he has kept all the commandments since his youth, and that he wants to do whatever is needed to inherit eternal life.

So Jesus challenges him to choose between God and money: "Go, sell your possessions, give the proceeds to the poor, and then join me and my disciples." Jesus is not asking him to become destitute, to have nothing to live on, or to beg for a living. Jesus is challenging him to join the group of disciples who are not in need because they share everything. It is a challenge to live a life of sharing with others.

But the rich young man is unable to do this. He is too attached to his possessions. He is enslaved to Mammon. And so he walks away sad.

And then third there are those who find themselves entangled in an idolatrous economic system without intending to worship Mammon themselves. Our economic system is structured in such a way that it serves Mammon and not people. "The market dictates," they say. Human beings are no longer free. We are caught up in an idolatrous financial structure. We become its victims. Let us look at some examples of this.

In Jesus' time the peasants were caught up in the system and became its victims. They had to pay a triple tax: to the Romans, to Herod, and to the Temple. They were quite simply unable to pay this triple tax, so they kept borrowing money and got into more and more debt, ending up with relentless anxiety about where their daily bread would come from. Many became beggars; others became petty thieves. They were trapped by the system.

In our time people are seduced by advertisements. They buy on credit or hire purchase [an installment plan] without understanding the consequences. When they can no longer pay the installments, the goods are repossessed or they borrow from the loan sharks. When they are unable to repay the loans and the exorbitant interest, they borrow from someone else to pay the loan shark, getting into worse and worse debt. Trapped again.

This is just one of the things that happen to people in a society dedicated to the worship of money. If wealth is the only goal worth pursuing, then we should not be surprised to hear of bribery, corruption, fraud, and rampant crime. And that is before we even begin to think about the unemployed, the poor, the destitute, and the starving millions. All of this is the inevitable result of idolatry—a society that worships money.

But what then is the alternative?

The Kingdom of God

The opposite of the worship of money is the worship of God. The individual who worships God will love his or her neighbors and be willing to share with them. The one who worships God will be free to share with others because he or she will be detached from money and possessions.

The worship of money has its roots in selfishness. It is the worship of one's ego. The worship of God is the very opposite of this. It is the selfless commitment to people, to love.

In social terms, we are talking about a *sharing* society, which is what the kingdom of God is about. The kingdom of God is a kingdom of love. And when it comes to money and possessions, love means being willing to share what we have. A kingdom of love is a kingdom of people who are willing to share with one another.

Sharing: that is Jesus' answer to the worship of Mammon. The Oikos Journey document calls it "God's economy." Jesus and his disciples, men and women, formed a sharing community. Judas had the common purse. But it is in the description of the first Christian community in the book of Acts that we have the clearest outline of what Jesus had in mind.

In Jerusalem, we are told, those who believed in Jesus "were of one mind and one heart and no one claimed private ownership of any possessions, but everything they owned was held in common . . . There was not a needy person among them, for as many as owned lands or houses sold them and brought the proceeds of what was sold. They laid it at the apostles' feet and it was distributed to each as any had need" (Acts 4:32–35).

This was nothing more than a small beginning—a mustard seed. It didn't grow very much except among the first monks and nuns, and in what we today call religious life. It was supposed to be the yeast or leaven that would influence the whole society. It would grow and develop into God's economy—the fullness of the kingdom of God.

We seem to be very far removed from anything like this today. Nevertheless, the beginnings of such communities of sharing are here in our midst, as the Oikos document points out. People in the churches do sometimes share with the poor, and the poor do sometimes share with one another. We must promote and extend this kind of thing.

A Practical Way Forward

The Oikos document has some suggestions about what we can do. The first is welfare work, like feeding the poor. The second is development work, like passing on skills and training to people in need. The third is to speak out prophetically against unjust structures. I would like to suggest two more practical actions.

The first concerns our entanglement in the system through the practice that is known as *consumerism*. We can fight against this by refusing to allow ourselves to be seduced by advertisements. We can try to avoid buying on credit or on hire purchase so that we spend each month's salary or allowance on paying off installments. We can begin to distinguish between what we really *need* and what we *want* because others have it or the ads say we must have it. If we play into the hands of our consumerist society, we are playing into the hands of an idolatrous system.

Let's avoid spending as far as we possibly can. Instead, let us save, save, save. When we do this, we undermine the idolatrous system. The more people there are who do it, the more the system will begin to fail.

The second practical action is to share wherever and whenever we possibly can. Act against selfishness and greed by forming cooperatives or other sharing groups. Prayer groups can also begin to share. Let's promote the value of sharing wherever we can. It undermines the selfish profit motive of the system. These suggestions would be nothing more than mustard seeds, but let's plant them and make them grow.

CHAPTER 13

Justice in the Bible

It should be made clear from the outset that the concept of justice that we find in the Bible is somewhat different from the concept of justice in Greek philosophy or in scholastic theology or in modern ideas about human rights. Justice in the Bible is not merely one of the four moral virtues. It includes the more limited meanings of justice that we find in philosophy and politics. Biblical justice is a much broader and more comprehensive concept. It covers the whole of morality—personal and social. All moral laws, principles, virtues, and actions are understood to be a matter of justice. As the famous Old Testament scholar Gerhard von Rad has said, "There is absolutely no concept in the Old Testament with so central a significance for all human relationships as that of justice" (*Old Testament Theology*, Vol. 1, Edinburgh: Oliver and Boyd, 1962, 1:370). In fact this is true not only of the Old Testament but of the whole Bible. In the words of another author, "It can be said without exaggeration that the Bible, taken as a whole, has one theme: The history of the revelation of God's justice" (H. H. Schrey, *The Biblical Doctrine of Justice and Law* [London: SCM Press, 1955, 50).

This is not immediately obvious in our translations of the Bible, partly because of the difficulty of translating the two Hebrew words *mispat* and *sedakah*. These two words have

---

This was originally a presentation delivered at a Dominican Conference in Caldwell, New Jersey, in July 1984. It was printed in the conference proceedings. The theme of the conference was "Justice and Truth Shall Meet."

much the same meaning, and in typical Hebrew fashion they are often used together. But because we have only one word for "justice" and because our word has a somewhat narrower meaning, in our English translations of the Bible these two Hebrew words are often translated by other words like "righteousness," "uprightness," "integrity," "honesty," "virtue," "holiness," and even "judgment." This is all very misleading and confusing, especially for the reader who does not know that all these English words refer to one and the same Hebrew concept of an all-embracing justice.

The translation of the corresponding Hebrew verbs is even more misleading. The Hebrew verbs mean literally "to do justice" or "to put wrongs right," but in our English Bible these Hebrew verbs are usually translated "to judge"! This makes us think of a judge who condemns and punishes people who have done wrong, whereas the Hebrew means someone who puts wrongs right by vindicating or rescuing the innocent. Thus, for example, the last judgment in the Bible means God's final act of justice when he puts right everything in the world that is wrong or unjust. And the judges in the book of Judges (Gideon, Samson, Deborah, Ehud, etc.) are not judges who sit in court hearing cases, they are the liberators of Israel who gather armies to go out and do justice by putting wrongs right—that is to say, liberating Israelites from their oppressors.

We could sum up, then, by saying that justice in the Bible (God's justice) is the state of affairs in which things are right or true—that is to say, that they are what they are supposed to be, what God wants them to be. And the activity of doing justice is the activity of putting right whatever is wrong in the world.

God and Justice

In the Bible, justice is first and foremost an attribute of God. God is just not only because God is fair and honest in all God's dealings with human beings but also because all God's activity is a matter of putting right what is wrong in the world, and all

God's laws and commandments are simply demanding that justice be done. In fact, justice is *the* distinguishing characteristic of the God of the Bible. Yahweh is the God of justice, and that precisely is how Yahweh differs from all the other gods that humans worship. The idols or false gods promote tyranny and oppression and demand unjust practices like human sacrifice and cultic prostitution. That is how the prophets knew that they were false gods or rather no gods at all. That is why the prophets were so concerned about idolatry. Idolatry was the worship of injustice and oppression, because the true God is justice.

We are accustomed to the Johannine statement that God is love. But it would be equally true to say that the fundamental and original revelation of the Bible is that there is a God who is justice and that this God's name is Yahweh—and indeed that there is no other god at all.

The revelation of Yahweh as the God of justice was made through Moses to a group of Hebrew slave workers in Egypt. They were suffering bitterly under the injustice of their Egyptian masters. Their oppression as workers was becoming worse and worse, and like all the other slaves and peasants of the ancient world, they had no hope at all of ever being liberated from injustice and oppression. As they would have understood it, there was no god to rescue them, no power in the world that might deliver them from bondage.

Gods were like kings, and kings were not interested in the problems of slaves. Pharaoh was called the son of god, and even the God of their Fathers, the God of Abraham, Isaac, and Jacob, would have been thought of, at this stage, as high and mighty, unconcerned about the plight of a few poor and insignificant Hebrews.

Then came Moses with the good news of a god who was moved by compassion for them in their plight; a god who was concerned about the sufferings of workers; a god who, unlike any other god or any human being, wanted to liberate slaves from their oppression. It was simply unheard of. Gods were not concerned about justice for the poor and oppressed. The newness of the revelation of Yahweh was precisely that he was the God of justice for the poor and oppressed, the liberator God. "I am Yahweh. I will free you of the burdens which the Egyptians lay on you. I will release you from slavery to them" (Exod. 6:6).

At first, the Hebrew slaves would not accept this new god, but after their miraculous escape from their oppressors, they attributed this success to the power of Yahweh and gradually came to realize that Yahweh was in fact the God of Abraham, Isaac, and Jacob (Exod. 6:2, 3) and indeed the creator God— the one and only God.

When we read the Bible in English, the unique nature of Yahweh is not easily detectable. This again is a question of translation. In all English Bibles, with the exception of the Jerusalem Bible, Yahweh is translated "Lord." The proper name of a unique and specially revealed God of justice and liberation is translated by a common, general, and masculine word: Lord. This translation makes complete nonsense of many a sentence in the Bible, especially when God is made to say that his name is Lord (e.g., Exod. 6:3).

Laws and the Just Society

During their wanderings in the desert, these emancipated Hebrew slaves began to discover the Torah, Yahweh's commandments about how people should live together in society. The Mosaic Law and especially the Ten Commandments were not simply a code for private and personal morality. They were the values, principles, and laws for the building of a just society. The aim of these liberated workers in the desert was not simply private morality or personal salvation. Their aim was the Promised Land, a land of milk and honey, a nation of justice and equality. They were not planning to set up another nation like Egypt. They were not about to repeat the same injustice, the same inequality, the same slavery and oppression. Many of their laws of fairness to strangers, widows, and orphans were explicitly motivated by the memory of their own unjust treatment in Egypt (e.g., Deut. 24:17–18).

The Mosaic Law is Yahweh's revelation of what would be just and what would not be just in the circumstances of those times. In Hebrew the commandments of the law are sometimes called the "justices" of the law. Thus, idolatry, blasphemy, adultery, and prostitution are all viewed as forms of injustice. Today we might want to nuance or even amend some of the patriarchal attitudes to women or some of the rather harsh forms of punishment, but what we have here in the Mosaic Law is the great religious ideal of justice and equality for all.

This becomes even clearer when we look at the society of the twelve tribes that they gradually constructed in the Promised Land. When they arrived in Canaan they found in the plains a series of city-states in which the kings and urban aristocracy oppressed the peasants, the people of the land. They were societies of inequality and exploitation. The liberated slaves from Egypt (or their descendants) brought hope of liberation to the peasants. They told the story of the exodus and of Yahweh, the God of justice and liberation. And so it was that all the poor and oppressed descendants of Jacob, both from Egypt and from Canaan, gathered together in the hill country, put their faith in Yahweh, and set out to destroy one by one the oppressive city-states of Canaan. In their place they set up the nation of the twelve tribes, the nation of Israel.

The outstanding characteristic of the nation of the twelve tribes was justice, and justice here means equality. In stark contrast to all the other nations of those times (the Gentiles), Israel was an egalitarian society. It had no king, no princes, no nobles or aristocracy. On the other hand, there were no slaves and no poor and oppressed classes of people. The book of Numbers tells us in great detail how all the land was carefully and meticulously divided so that each family would have an equal portion (e.g., Num. 33:54; Josh. 13:21). There were no rich and no poor.

For nearly two hundred years, Israel was indeed the most extraordinary nation in the history of humankind. Not for nothing was this nation called the "chosen nation of the God of justice." As a nation it was God's own creation. Unfortunately it did not last.

Inequality set in as some families fell into more and more debt and sold more and more of their land to pay their mounting debts and eventually, in some cases, sold themselves as slaves. Yahweh was not pleased with this. Everyone knew it. So the law of the Jubilee Year was introduced to put right what had gone wrong. According to this law, every fifty years the nation was to emancipate all slaves, cancel all debts, and restore all land to its original owners.

We are not told whether they were ever able to put this law into effect. Nevertheless, it stands there in Leviticus 25 as a great witness to the concern of the God of justice in whom we believe. In the words of the *Jerome Biblical Commentary*, it was "a social blueprint founded on the deeply religious concepts of justice and equality . . . its spirit of appreciation for personal rights and human dignity synthesizes much of Old Testament teaching."

Kings and Prophets

The death blow to this egalitarian society of the twelve tribes was the introduction of the monarchy, the appointment of kings in Israel. Yahweh tells Samuel what the results will be: inequality, injustice, oppression, and slavery. "He will take your sons and assign them to his chariotry and cavalry and they will run in front of his chariot. . . . He will make them plow *his* land and harvest *his* harvest and make his weapons of war. . . . He will take your daughters as perfumers, cooks and bakers. He will take the best of your fields . . . and give them to his officials. He will tax your crops and vineyards to provide for his officials. . . . You will become his slaves" (1 Sam. 8:11–17).

But the people persisted in asking for a king in order to become powerful like other nations. God eventually allowed it, and slowly but surely the predicted results all came true: first, Saul with his army; then David (though he was a somewhat benevolent dictator); and finally Solomon with his wives, slaves, and incredible wealth. The Hebrews had now come full circle: one of their own sons had now become an absolute monarch just like Pharaoh. The people were once again enslaved and oppressed.

Yahweh's struggle for justice becomes a struggle against the kings of Judah and Israel, just as it had once been a struggle against the pharaohs of Egypt and the kings of the Canaanite plains. And now the messengers and agents of God's justice are the prophets. The period of the prophets and the period of the kings coincide. The prophets and the kings go together—as adversaries.

We all know the prophets' impassioned plea to the nation that it turn back from its headlong plunge into disaster, doom, and destruction, and that it come back to Yahweh, to the exodus, the desert, and justice. But the prophets did not see it as a matter of returning to the past, but as a historical project of building a new justice for the future, a new covenant, a new spirit, and a new age.

The new justice was inaugurated by Jesus.

The New Justice

Jesus is the just one (Acts 3:13; 7:52). He embodies, incarnates, and reveals the justice of God (Rom. 1:16–17; 3:21–22; 4:25), and he inaugurates the new historical project of building a just world, what he calls the reign of God and its justice (Matt. 6:33).

Some Christians think that the New Testament says very little about justice and that love replaces justice as the fundamental and all-embracing virtue. But it is only possible to think like that if justice is thought of as one virtue among many.

The New Testament is all about justice, and the word occurs very frequently if you remember that "righteousness" means "justice" and that "justification" means making someone or something just, putting right what was wrong.

Jesus made it quite clear from the start that he had not come to abolish the law but to fulfill it. In other words, he had not come to abolish God's demand for justice but to fulfill that demand. This Jesus does by trying to take the people, and especially the scribes and Pharisees, beyond their present, very narrow ideas of what is just and what is not. "Unless your justice goes beyond that of the scribes and Pharisees, you will never enter the kingdom of heaven" (Matt. 5:17–20).

Jesus says this at the beginning of the Sermon on the Mount. He then proceeds to take examples from the law to deepen them, to go beyond them and fulfill them—to preach the new justice. To illustrate this, we might look at what he does about the commandments against killing and adultery. Basically he says our concern should be not only with the external act of murder or adultery but also with the interior act. You could say that he was telling us not to commit "murder of the heart" or "adultery of the heart." Jesus is interiorizing the law, interiorizing justice. He is asking about one's motive for doing justice. What is your motive for not committing adultery or not killing someone you hate? Fear of being caught?

This new justice comes spontaneously from the heart. It is a justice of the heart, motivated by a passion for justice. Now this passion for justice is what we generally call compassion for people.

Compassion, as you know, means "feeling with" people, especially people in need, suffering people. Compassion was very important as the starting point for Jesus. He was moved by compassion for the poor, the sick, and the outcasts.

In short, Jesus' way of deepening and renewing justice was to bring in compassion as the heart of justice, as the motive for a passionate devotion to justice.

Justice and Love

One could say that this new justice is love, and Jesus himself calls it love; but then we must never forget that, for Jesus, love is a commandment and therefore a matter of justice. God *commands* us to love our neighbor. That makes it a matter of justice because now my neighbor has the *right* to be loved. Love is no longer a matter of doing my neighbor a favor out of the generosity of my heart. This kind of condescending and paternalistic love is rejected today by people who say, "Don't give us your 'charity.' Give us our rights." True love, however, *is* a matter of giving people their rights.

Feeding the hungry, giving drink to the thirsty, clothing the naked, and visiting the imprisoned and the sick are *works of justice*. That is how the Bible sees it (e.g., Matt. 25:37). We tend to see them as *works of mercy*, and what we mean is that they are an optional extra for which you will be highly rewarded. The Bible might also call them "works of mercy" but would understand that to mean the same as "works of justice." Justice and mercy (compassion) meet. They are coterminous.

But what is new about this in the teaching of Jesus? Do we not already have references to "mercy" and "compassion" in the Old Testament? Yes, but in the Old Testament mercy and compassion were thought of as almost entirely attributes of God alone. Very few humans were compassionate, even if some of them sometimes did what was right and just and true. The new thing in the new justice of Jesus is that he brings divine compassion into the historical project of building a just world. "Be compassionate as your Father is compassionate" (Luke 6:36). Jesus challenges us to imitate Yahweh, who was moved by compassion for the slaves in Egypt and who therefore set out to put these wrongs right.

Compassion and justice are of the very nature of God—so much so that Jeremiah can say that the practice of justice *is* the knowledge of God (Jer. 22:16). If we do not practice justice, we have no experience of God because God is justice. John says this of love. If we do not love, we have no experience of God because God is love (1 John 4:7–8). And he says something very similar of justice, too (1 John 2:29). There is no dichotomy between justice and love in the Bible.

But all of this faces us with a very serious problem. If the practice of justice is the experience of God, we are surrounded every day by people who know nothing of God. They may indeed profess to believe in God, but they are in practice atheists. We have, it seems, a great deal of religion, ritual, and prayer from which God is absent because justice is absent. Moreover, according to the prophets this kind of ritual and prayer is hypocritical, blasphemous, and something that makes God very angry. Isaiah expresses this very strongly and unequivocally in his opening chapter.

> "What are your endless sacrifices to me,"
>   says Yahweh.
> "I am sick of burnt offerings of rams
> and the fat of calves.
> I take no pleasure in the blood
> of bulls and lambs and goats. . . .
>
> "When you stretch out your hands I turn my
>   eyes away.
> You may multiply your prayers, I shall not
>   be listening. . . .
>
> "Take your wrong-doing out of my sight.
> Cease doing evil.
> Learn to do good.
> Search for justice.
> Discipline the violent.
> Be just to the orphan.
> Plead for the widow." (Isa. 1:11, 15, 17)

CHAPTER 14

Personal Liberation

The liberation we struggled for in South Africa, liberation from the social structure called apartheid, was a form of *social liberation*. What we struggled against was an oppressive racial structure that had to be dismantled and replaced by a democratic social system. This liberation struggle was remarkably successful. We now have a constitution that is second to none and a democratically elected government that has transformed the country in many ways.

But our liberation is not complete. We now live, like most other people in the world, under an oppressive economic system. The next form of social liberation will be economic. But that will take time—much more time and selfless commitment.

What we face today, however, is a different kind of crisis. Our more immediate crisis has to do with the personal behavior of individuals or perhaps we could say misbehavior. I want to call it "antisocial behavior." My argument in this talk is that what we now need is a new struggle—a concerted struggle for *personal liberation*, for ourselves and for others. But let me begin with a brief description of the present crisis.

The Present Crisis

We have all been shocked by the amount of violence that characterizes life in South Africa today: murders, family mur-

---

This comes from a multidisciplinary public lecture delivered at the invitation of the University of South Africa in May 2008.

ders, family suicides, muti [medicine] murders, the killing of children and even babies. We fear criminals who will kill for a cell phone. Even more revealing is the amount of domestic violence, rape, and child abuse in our country. At school, too, there is an increase, it seems, in bullying, fighting, and even murder. We read about taxi violence, police violence, strikers who become violent, and vigilantes who take the law into their own hands. The net result is fear, suspicion, high walls, and barbed wire.

Theft has also become endemic. We think immediately of the heists, burglaries, car hijackings, and bank robberies, as well as corruption, bribery, and fraud. But there is also the petty theft of tools and goods from the workplace. Almost everyone does it. Greed is rampant. The recent price fixing of bread is but one example of how greed exploits the consumer and especially the poor. The result here is the feeling that nobody can be trusted.

Anthony Altbeker wrote a book about South Africa titled *A Country at War with Itself*. He was writing about crime, but I think there are other ways in which we are at war with one another. We are plagued by conflictual relationships. Racism and racial prejudices remain. They are no longer structural or constitutional, but they still plague our personal relationships. And now we seem to have developed numerous other conflictual relationships: rivalries, backstabbing, and personalized power struggles as in the so-called succession battle in the ANC—not to mention the conflict between municipal counselors, civil servants, and even nurses on the one hand and the public they are supposed to serve. We seem to be losing the spirit of service and helpfulness.

Another source of conflict is the present culture of blame. When things go wrong we tend to find someone to blame: the government, the president, the ANC, the police, or the media. Pointing fingers is seldom helpful. It just increases the war we seem to be waging against one another. I would see this kind of behavior as also antisocial.

The fourth category of antisocial behavior as I understand it is the desire for instant gratification—wanting the quick fix with no thought for the future. Instead of saving for the future, people spend recklessly, buy on hire purchase [an installment plan], and borrow money with no idea how they will ever be able to pay it back. The loan sharks exploit this, so that we now have a serious consumer debt crisis.

Heavy drinking, drug abuse, and drunken driving would be further examples of instant gratification that give no thought to the consequences. Hence our high incidence of road accidents. It is not surprising, then, that we give so little thought to the crisis of global warming and the destruction of the environment. Who cares? The widespread unwillingness to cooperate with Eskom to save electricity is yet another symptom of our antisocial attitudes.

In conclusion, every day I hear people saying, "This is not the society we struggled for. This is not the kind of society people sacrificed their lives for. Where did it go wrong? What happened to the values of the struggle?"

How then are we to understand what is happening in South Africa today? And what should our response be?

Responses

The Sociological Response

Sociologists speak about deviant behavior. It is defined as behavior that deviates from the rules or norms of society. That is not the issue here. Some of the things mentioned above may be deviant, but much of it is regarded as perfectly normal. Part of the problem is that many of the norms of the past seem to have little credence today. So it is regarded as perfectly normal, for example, to take a bribe or to steal from the workplace, and if you do not do so, you are just odd or out of touch.

In some countries the term "antisocial behavior" refers to

such things as vandalism and littering. The antisocial behavior I am referring to is something much more serious than that. What we are witnessing in South Africa today is the collapse of all our cultures (African, Western, and Asian), as well as our various religious principles and commandments. The moral values and the social norms of the past are no longer accepted by most people, and especially not by the youth.

The American writer Gil Bailie calls it "cultural and social disintegration." It is a worldwide phenomenon. South Africa is simply an advanced example of it. This is our challenge today, just as apartheid was our challenge some years ago.

The Political Response

The political response would be to make more laws and strengthen law enforcement. Or change the government or the leadership. In other words, deal with it as a structural problem that calls for a structural solution. But I really don't believe that it is as simple as that.

The Moral Response

Many see the problem as a case of moral degeneration and advocate some kind of moral regeneration. The government's program of moral regeneration is a brave attempt to do this, and President Thabo Mbeki in his Freedom Day address revisited the need for moral renewal. But noble as it is in itself, the Moral Regeneration Movement has had very little success.

It might have worked earlier in an age when people still believed in moral principles and ethical values. The postmodern generation does not want to have any moral laws imposed upon them. "Don't tell us what to do and what not to do. We want to decide for ourselves. We want freedom. We want to take responsibility for our own lives."

Anyone who has tried to teach moral principles or ethical

values to young people today knows that you cannot appeal to any kind of authority at all. Today's youth have to discover these things for themselves. That is one of the results of the breakdown of cultures and religions.

The Response of Spirituality

The kind of response that I wish to argue for would be spiritual and personal. Spirituality enables us to discover who we are and how we can live in peace, joy, and freedom. It entails a radical, personal transformation and a struggle for authenticity and truthfulness. Spirituality is the road to personal freedom.

One of the advantages of this approach is that it not only recognizes that many people in our society today need to be personally liberated but that I, too, need personal liberation, even if I do not engage in some of the really serious antisocial behavior that others do. The spiritual approach is not a self-righteous approach.

We are now in a position to begin unpacking this idea of personal liberation. But before I do so, let me say that the obvious example of this in South Africa is Madiba. He struggled for the social liberation of South Africa, but he is also a grand example of a man who is free in himself, free from any kind of bitterness or pettiness or hypocrisy or self-aggrandizement. He may not be perfect, but he is an excellent example of personal freedom. There have been and still are many others—for example, the great Walter Sisulu—but most others are not as well known as Mandela.

Personal Freedom

The first and most obvious question is "Freedom from what?" The short answer is "Freedom from ourselves." We oppress ourselves, or more accurately, we are oppressed by our impulsive desires and by our selfish egos.

Impulsive Desires

As we know only too well, our impulsive desires need to be curbed and controlled by self-discipline. The impulse to have sex, to eat, to drink, to sleep, and to react angrily and even violently cannot be allowed to control us without disastrous consequences. We need some measure of self-control; otherwise we become slaves of our short-term, thoughtless impulses. Either we control these impulses, or they control us—and if they control us, we are not free.

The first step toward personal freedom, then, is self-control. In the circumstances of South Africa today, with the breakdown of cultural and religious norms, self-control is crucial. But it needs to be seen as an act of freedom and not as another form of oppression. If I cannot control my impulses, then I am an oppressed slave.

Much of what we see happening around us are blind and impulsive reactions: killing, suicide, rape, child abuse, wife beating, drunkenness, overeating, and road rage, for example.

Discipline and self-control contribute to our personal freedom, but it is not the whole story. Some of the antisocial behavior we experience, including our own, is premeditated and deliberate. We are oppressed not only by our impulsive desires but also by our selfish egos.

Egocentricity

Psychologists and psychotherapists use the word "ego" in a variety of ways. I use the word as it is understood in all the literature on spirituality and increasingly in psychology, too. In this context, my ego is my selfish self, my self-centeredness. It refers to my *false self,* which is to say, a false image of who I am. And it is false because it is an image of myself as the center of the world.

I am not the center of the world. That is an illusion. My ego then is not my true self.

When I judge everything and everybody in relation to me and only me, I have myself and the whole world out of perspective. When I see everything and everybody as mere objects for my use, I have lost touch with reality. I have become egocentric. I have become blind to the needs and feelings of others. I also have lost contact with nature, the earth, and the universe of which I am a part.

We can easily recognize egocentricity in others. We say they have big egos or swollen egos. We can see how they are always in conflict with other people, how they hurt and harm others in one way or another. Their swollen egos make them loveless, heartless, and even cruel.

This kind of selfish behavior is generally curbed by law enforcement, cultural taboos, or religious commandments. But when all our cultures are breaking down, when religious faith is weakening, and when law enforcement agents can no longer cope, selfish people engage more easily in antisocial behavior, from murder to rape to crime and child abuse or any number of other possible selfish pursuits.

We continue to need curbs to control antisocial behavior, but more important still we need to tackle the problem at its roots: our slavery to our egos, to our illusions about ourselves. This would be the process I am calling personal liberation.

True Freedom

With all the spiritual writers and all the wisdom traditions and faiths, I am saying that true freedom is not freedom *of* the ego but freedom *from* the ego. Personal freedom is often thought of as the freedom of the ego to do whatever my selfishness dictates. But what we are talking about here is freedom from the ego, from the tyranny of selfishness.

Freedom of the ego is the freedom to exploit, kill, victimize, marginalize, or just ignore others when it is for my benefit or the benefit of my group. On the other hand, freedom from my ego is the freedom to love, serve, and care for others, unhindered by my own hang-ups, obsessions, and selfishness. It is the freedom to pursue the common good. This is, of course, easier said than done. It is a great ideal, but how practical is it? Freedom from one's ego obviously takes time. Short-term measures like law enforcement and moral laws are needed, but there will be no lasting peace until we set out on this course of personal liberation. Nor is it something that goes against our nature as human beings. All human beings want to love and be loved, to have inner freedom and peace.

The first step in this direction would be self-knowledge. To become free, what we need is not more rules and laws, but more self-knowledge.

Self-Knowledge

The struggle for social liberation, as we well know, includes the need for conscientization or awareness raising. People need to be made aware of the causes of their poverty and oppression. They have to discover for themselves that they are oppressed by unjust social structures. We call this conscientization.

The struggle for personal liberation also begins with a form of conscientization or awareness raising. We need to become aware of ourselves, our motives, our rationalizations, our prejudices, our obsessions—in short, our egos. We cannot begin to be liberated from this inner slavery until we become aware of it in ourselves. Hence the emphasis upon self-knowledge in all psychology, philosophy, religion, and spirituality. The psychologist Neville Symington speaks of self-knowledge as "the foundation-stone of mental health." According to the Gospel of Thomas, Jesus said, "Those who know everything else but do not know themselves, know nothing." The practical starting point on the road to personal transformation, then, is self-knowledge, self-awareness.

Some Practical Considerations

• If self-knowledge is the beginning of personal liberation, then the psychologist, therapist, or professional counselor obviously has an important role to play. Such professionals help people to become aware of what has been buried or hidden in the subconscious. However, only the privileged few can afford this kind of therapy. Nor is it necessary for everyone.

• The family has a role to play here. Parenting for self-control, self-awareness, and inner freedom is a great challenge. Parents need to find ways of helping one another. The biggest problem here is that too many parents have very little self-knowledge and are not personally free.

• There is also an urgent need to introduce young people to the practice of self-criticism and self-appreciation at school. It would be one of the most important elements in the Life Skills course that is a feature of our new Outcomes-Based Education. It is also important to develop some appreciation of ethical norms and values at school, but my point is that self-knowledge is crucial for anyone who will later be challenged to be unselfish and personally free.

• Given the present crisis of social disintegration, rehabilitation programs for criminals in our prisons are of crucial importance. Here, too, efforts could be made to help the prisoner get to know himself or herself and to value inner peace and inner freedom. I do not believe that this task would be as impossible as it might at first sight appear to be.

• The government has tried to address the present crisis of social disintegration by setting up the Moral Regeneration Movement. As I said earlier, it does not appear to be making much progress. I would think that this movement should meet with sociologists, political scientists, theologians, educators, and with practitioners of spirituality—with a view to developing a liberation ethics or morality.

• Then there is the university. Multidisciplinary research, lectures, and debates are needed. (The present lecture might be an example of that.) What is to my mind particularly important is the inclusion of those who know the spiritual traditions that are gaining in prominence and popularity today. This is not a matter of arguing about religious dogma, but rather a matter of taking spiritual experience seriously.

• That brings me finally to religion: our religious institutions and spiritual movements. Self-knowledge is part of what religious faiths enable a person to do. They can and often do lead believers to a more honest awareness of themselves and their relation to others. They teach people to love one another and have compassion on those who suffer.

But why then do religious institutions and spiritual movements seem to have so little success these days? My argument is that what the religions teach does not appear to be personally liberating, and above all the God they preach does not seem to be a liberating God but an oppressive one.

There is the challenge especially to those of us who are theologians: to clarify the role that God plays in the process of personal transformation and inner freedom. We once did that in relation to social liberation.

And that is why I wrote my book *Jesus Today: A Spirituality of Radical Freedom.* It is my attempt to show how Jesus' spirituality of radical freedom is relevant today, in South Africa and elsewhere.

CHAPTER 15

Structures of Sin

One of the features of *Sollicitudo Rei Socialis* (*SRS*), the 1987 encyclical of Pope John Paul II, was the introduction of a new phrase into the language of the social teaching of the church, namely, "structures of sin." We quote from paragraph 36.

> It is important to note therefore that a world which is divided into blocs, sustained by rigid ideologies, and in which instead of interdependence and solidarity different forms of imperialism hold sway, can only be a world subject to structures of sin. . . .
>
> If the present situation can be attributed to difficulties of various kinds, it is not out of place to speak of "structures of sin." . . .
>
> "Sin" and "structures of sin" are categories that are seldom applied to the situation of the contemporary world. However, one cannot easily gain a profound understanding of the reality that confronts us unless we give a name to the root of the evils which afflict us.

The social reality that is being referred to here was previously known as "social sin." This has always been a somewhat am-

---

This first appeared as an article published in 2007 in *Angelicum*, the academic journal of the Pontifical University of St. Thomas Aquinas in Rome.

biguous term. All sin is personal. Only individual persons can be guilty of sin. A society or social group cannot sin in any literal sense of the word. What do we mean then by "social sin"? Is it the sum total of the personal sins of a social group? Or does it refer to personal sins that have social consequences? Or both?

Speaking of social sins as structures of sin adds an interesting new dimension. It seems to imply that some social structures are themselves sinful.

The concept of unjust social structures has been with us for a long time. One of the features of liberation theology in all its forms has been and still is the development of a theological understanding of unjust structures and of the struggles to change them.[1] Is this what is meant by structures of sin? In what sense can unjust structures be spoken of as sinful?

A notorious example of unjust structures in the twentieth century was South Africa's policy of racial discrimination known as apartheid. During the 1980s I tried to reflect on the sinfulness of the structures of apartheid. Where was the sin? Who was guilty? I published my conclusions in a book entitled *God in South Africa*. In this essay I make use of some of those ideas.

But what I have also found particularly relevant in writing this essay on the structures of sin was the unpublished doctoral thesis of my late colleague Bernard Connor. It was a comprehensive study of social sin titled "Sin, Self and Society." I am indebted to Bernard for many of the thoughts in this essay.

The place to start, though, is sociology. What are the sociologists saying about the nature of a social structure, about how social structures are generated and reproduced, and how they change? Only after that can we explore the relationship between social structures and sin.

---

[1] See, for example, Gustavo Gutiérrez, *A Theology of Liberation: History, Politics and Salvation*, trans. Caridad Inda and John Eagleson (Maryknoll, N.Y.: Orbis Books, 1973).

Social Structures

There is no agreed-upon definition of a social structure. Sociologists or social theorists base their understanding of social structures on their different social theories. While recognizing this, the well-known *Unwin Hyman Dictionary of Sociology* provides us with two closely related meanings for the word "social structure": (1) "any relatively enduring pattern or interrelationship of social elements," and (2) "the more or less enduring pattern of social arrangements within a particular society, group or social organization." We could sum this up by saying that a social structure is a pattern of social relationships. Examples of this structure would include the family, the nation, the cultural group, a religion or church, an economic system, a racist society, and a patriarchal culture. They all involve particular patterns of social relations that are expressed as laws, rules, customs, traditions, values, practices, authority structures, and power relations.

While the study of these patterns has been one of the defining features of sociology, many theologians and activists have also been involved in the practical analysis of social structures. They, too, describe what they are doing as social analysis. What matters, though, is the type of social theory we make use of to understand how these structures are produced and reproduced, and how they change. These theories can be roughly divided into three kinds.[2] The first is that social structures themselves are the determining factor rather than individual human agency. This would be the general Marxist tendency, although it would not be true to say that all Marxists exclude free human agency. Their emphasis, however, is on the material conditions that give rise to structures and reproduce them or lead to their transformation.

---

[2]Anthony Giddens, *The Constitution of Society: Outline of the Theory of Structuration* (Cambridge: Polity Press, 1984), 206–21.

The second theory is that social structures are produced, re-produced, and changed almost entirely by human agency. This tendency would discount the influence that social structures can have on the behavior of human beings. The emphasis is on human freedom. Social conditioning is not taken very seriously. This kind of theory might be described as the liberal, individualist tendency.

The third kind of theory would be concerned to show how social structures and human agency are both involved in the construction, the reproduction, and the transformation of society. This kind of theory is receiving the most attention these days, and the social theorist who offers us the most profound insights into this matter is undoubtedly Anthony Giddens.

In his groundbreaking work on what he calls structuration, *The Constitution of Society*, Giddens warns us about reifying social structures, treating them as objective things that can exist independently of human agency.

This (patterning of social relations) is often naively conceived of in terms of visual imagery, akin to the skeleton or morphology of an organism or to the girders of a building. Such conceptions are closely related to the dualism of subject and social object: "structure" here appears as "external" to human action.[3]

In other words we should not visualize a social structure as a kind of building that remains standing after it has been vacated by its inhabitants. It is more like the course, direction, or shape of a river. The water and its cascading patterns are inseparable. You cannot really have a pattern without something that is being patterned. Nor can you have a flowing river or a fountain that has no shape or direction—no structure.[4]

---

[3]Ibid., 16.
[4]Bernard F. Connor, *The Difficult Traverse: From Amnesty to Reconciliation*, (Pietermaritzburg: Cluster Publications, 1998), 86.

Between social structure and human agency, there is what I would call a dialectical relationship. While on the one hand social structures are produced and reproduced by human agency, on the other hand human action (or inaction) is powerfully influenced by social structures. The structures can constrain or enable people to act or to refrain from acting,[5] but they are not deterministic, depriving human beings of all freedom.

We have all been socialized into one social system or another. We are all, to a greater or lesser extent, socially conditioned. But we can become aware of that, and then it becomes possible to transcend our conditioning and to change the social structures of which we are a part. Human agency in producing, reproducing, or changing a social structure varies enormously from person to person and from time to time. Bernard Connor describes something of the complexity of the agency of white people in the social structures of apartheid.

> What each person knew, tried to discover or deliberately avoided finding out varied from one individual to another. While some spoke out, others denied both to self and others that anything was seriously amiss. A person's chances of grasping what was happening differed according to locality, job, access to information: each of these was partly a matter of choice and partly of circumstances. How each person used his or her power to influence events—for good or ill—likewise varied from one individual to another.[6]

Structural Change

Before the French Revolution, the idea that the structures of a society could be changed by human agency was largely unknown. You could replace one ruler or king by another, but

---

[5] Giddens, *Constitution of Society*, 169–80.
[6] Connor, *Difficult Traverse*, 92–93.

the monarchical structure remained. You could rejoice in having a more benevolent chief than before, but the tribal structure continued. One ruler could be more just and fair than another, but the system was the same. Peasants could rebel against the aristocracy, but the feudal system of serfs and aristocrats was regarded as unchangeable, and social mobility from one social status to another was regarded as impossible. For most people the social structure was divinely ordained—hence the principle known as "the divine right of kings."

The French Revolution changed all of this—at least in principle. Social structures could be changed because they had been constructed by human beings, are reproduced by human beings, and can be changed by human beings—for better or for worse. The Russian Revolution demonstrated the same point, whatever one may think of the results. Social structures can be changed.[7]

A particularly good example would be the abolition of slavery. Before William Wilberforce and others succeeded in changing the social structure of slavery by persuading the British government to change the laws that allowed for slavery, it was regarded as impossible to have a successful economy without slave labor. Even St. Paul did not think that the division of society into slaves and masters could be changed. Jesus had done away with the distinction between masters and slaves, and Christians would have to treat one another as equals. But it was assumed that until the kingdom comes, human society would continue to be structured in this way.

Colonialism was another structure that was taken for granted until the colonized peoples of the world began to struggle for their independence. Other examples of structural change would be the dismantling of the structures of racism in South Africa and the gradual dismantling of patriarchy and sexism. Almost all the many different struggles for justice in the world

---

[7]Albert Nolan, *Jesus Today: A Spirituality of Radical Freedom* (Maryknoll, N.Y.: Orbis Books, 2006), 28–29.

today are seen as struggles to change unjust social structures. The World Social Forum that brings all these struggles and movements together sees the common denominator as the belief that another world is possible.[8]

Two things should be noted about structural change, however. First, structures do not always change for the better. Sometimes we witness a coup d'état that changes a country from a democracy into a military dictatorship. Second, there are no universal laws about how structures change.[9] Sometimes structures become dysfunctional and unsustainable, as apartheid did in South Africa. But even then they do not change of themselves. Human action is needed. Moreover, what makes some structures unsustainable and others not, is not always the same. There seem to be numerous variables here.

Unjust Structures

If the principal aim of social justice work today is structural change, then it is because we now recognize that social structures themselves can be unjust. But what does that mean?

Everyone can now recognize that apartheid, for example, was an unjust social structure. Why? Because it discriminated against black people and favored whites. It was unjust because the system itself benefited some people and not others. In fact, the victims of apartheid were oppressed and suffered untold cruelty, deprivation, and humiliation. The effects of this structure were so devastating, so hurtful, and so harmful to human beings that it was labeled a crime against humanity.

What should be noticed here is that the injustice of this social structure was manifested in, and measured by, its effect upon people. It was unjust because it led to so much pain and suffering for the majority in the country. There were human

---

[8]Ibid., 34–35.
[9]Giddens, *Constitution of Society*, 228–43.

agents, of course, who produced and reproduced this system, and they were guilty to a greater or lesser degree. But what made the system unjust was not that. It was the effect that such a pattern of social relations had upon people.[10]

The same can be said of our present economic structures worldwide. They are unjust because they benefit a few and condemn billions of others to poverty and destitution. That the poor get poorer and the rich richer is inherent in the very structure of this economy. It is the only way this system can work, not because the system upholds the right to private property, but because the profit motive that keeps it going puts no limits on private ownership. There are no limits to what any one person or corporation can accumulate while others have nothing and are starving to death. The system is so structured that one person can legally own a thousand times more than he or she will ever need, while it is illegal for a poor person to steal a loaf of bread. That is unjust—structurally unjust.

Some say that there is no alternative. We have to be practical and realistic. That is, of course, a lie, but in any case it does not prove that the economic structures as such are just and fair.

Others say that the inequalities have to be made up by individual or corporate acts of kindness in helping the poor, or that poor relief is the business of government. But none of this detracts from the truth that the structures themselves are unfair and detrimental to human well-being.

It is not only the poor who suffer. The system can only flourish by continuing to grow, whether there is a need for further growth or not—somewhat like a cancerous cell. This leads to the creation of needs by means of extravagant advertising and the encouragement of consumerism. The hurt and harm to human beings seem to have no limits.

But then who is guilty? Where is the sin?

---

[10]Albert Nolan, *God in South Africa* (Cape Town: David Philip, 1988), 34–38, 96.

Structures of Sin

Once we introduce the concept of sin, we are asking about human guilt. As we have already noted, social structures cannot sin. Only individual human beings can be regarded as guilty of sin. In what sense, then, can we speak of sinful structures or structures of sin?

According to our traditional moral theology, three elements are to be considered in any sin: knowledge, consent, and matter. We say that for a sin to be serious or "mortal," there must be full knowledge, full consent, and grave matter. Guilt is constituted by the full knowledge and full consent, or rather the degree of guilt involved depends upon the degree of knowledge and consent in the sinner.[11]

However, there has been in our moral teaching the tendency to emphasize the degree of guilt involved rather than the gravity of the matter. The gravity of the matter is the amount of harm done to oneself and/or others. In other words, our tendency has been to regard a sin as very serious when someone does it with full knowledge and full consent, even if the matter itself is trivial in the sense that it does no real harm to anyone. The sinner here is patently guilty even if the act is of no great consequence.

On the other hand, when someone did not act with full knowledge and full consent, when they did not know what they were doing and did not intend the consequences, we tend to exonerate them no matter what the consequences of their act might have been. If, as a result of the actor's behavior, many millions of people were killed but the person involved cannot be blamed for it, we tend to think there is nothing wrong. But grave matter remains grave matter even if full knowledge and full consent are absent, even if there is no guilt at all. You might want to say in such cases that even if there is no sin involved,

---

[11]Ibid., 38, 96.

because all the conditions for a sin have not been realized, nevertheless we have a very serious problem. Many people have been made to suffer—albeit unintentionally.

The traditional way of describing this is to say that what we have here is a material sin rather than a formal sin. The matter is grave and needs to be taken seriously, even if the formality of guilt is not present.

How does this apply to what we call unjust structures, sinful structures, and structures of sin? We could say that such structures are materially sinful because of the pain and suffering they inflict upon people. They constitute what one might call very grave matter. But then, what about guilt? When we introduce the word "sin" and when Pope John Paul II introduces it in *SRS*, the intention is to emphasize the element of guilt.

Who Is Guilty?

Only individual persons can be guilty. Only free human agents can act with full knowledge and full consent. With regard to unjust structures, then, all those who knowingly and willingly built the structures by making the laws, designing the policies, fabricating the rationalizations for it, and promoting its false values would be guilty. But not only them. All those who reproduce the system daily by knowingly and willingly benefiting from its injustices and making excuses for their conformity to the demands and temptations of the unjust arrangements and relations are also guilty (Nolan 1988, 90). This would include those who do nothing. The system continues to be reproduced by those who sin by omission. They are also guilty.

So, behind and within structures of sin are numerous individuals who are personally guilty. They are guilty of producing and reproducing sinful structures. In the words of *SRS*,

It is not out of place to speak of "structures of sin," which are rooted in personal sin, and thus always linked to the *concrete acts* of individuals who introduce these structures, consolidate them and make them difficult to remove. And thus they grow stronger, spread and become the source of other sins, and so influence people's behavior. (36)

The problem, though, is that it is very difficult to pinpoint this guilt. Even if we could name those who originally introduced the sinful structures and even if we could say who is reproducing the system today, we would still have difficulty deciding to what extent they knew what they were doing and consented to the consequences. Was there full knowledge and full consent? Who will judge that? And is it at all necessary to find out who is to blame and how guilty they might be? Is that not something we can leave to Almighty God and the consciences of individuals?

What matters is that unjust structures be dismantled and replaced. We do not do this by going around finding people to blame. We do it first of all by becoming conscious ourselves of the grave matter we are dealing with here, and of the pain and suffering that is caused by such unjust structures. Having become aware of this ourselves, the next step would be to make as many others as possible fully conscious of it— especially those who have acted without full knowledge and full consent.

This is the process we call "conscientization." It means making everyone conscious of the structures, how they work, how we unwittingly reproduce them and what we could do to change them. Even those who do not benefit from the system or those who are seriously oppressed by it need to be conscientized; in fact, it is especially they who need to become aware of why they suffer so much in this situation.

The aim of conscientization is not to make anyone feel guilty but to challenge everyone to change the structures. What we all need to feel responsible for is allowing any unjust structure to continue unchallenged.

Social Structures and Temptation

There is yet another way in which social structures can be related to sin. They tempt people to sin.[12] Those who benefit from unjust structures of one kind or another will be seriously tempted to follow its laws, customs, values, and practices. Such structures legitimate sins of discrimination and justify our indulgence in unjust practices. Structures of sin make it difficult for us to see anything wrong with our selfishness. In fact, they make what is wrong appear to be right—at least for those who benefit from the way society is structured.

Many of us have been socialized into unjust systems. As I mentioned earlier, we have been socially conditioned. The tendency then is to follow the crowd, which is to say, to follow those who benefit from the system. Swimming against the stream can be very difficult, even dangerous. The temptation is to conform.

Some people have so little awareness of anything at all that they are almost incapable of making a personal choice against their social group and its expectations. They are tempted, and they fall for the temptation without even stopping to reflect upon what is happening. They reproduce the system unwittingly. Here again, what is required is conscientization. Everybody needs to be made aware of what is happening, especially of the insidious way in which some of us are tempted by unjust social structures. Conscientization leads to what we call an option for the poor.

The Option for the Poor

There seems to me to be a considerable amount of confusion about what it means to take an option for the poor. The

---

[12]Ibid., 92–95.

confusion becomes obvious when one hears people speaking about a *preferential* option for the poor or, as the encyclical *SRS* expresses it, "a love of preference for the poor" (*optionem pauperum et amorem potiorem erga eos*).

The option for the poor has nothing to do with loving the poor more than the rich or preferring the poor to the rich. As disciples of Jesus we are committed to loving everyone unconditionally, whether they be rich or poor, sinners or saints, guilty or not. While Jesus was closer to some people than to others and had some good friends, his great strength was that he loved everyone with the same boundless love. He did not prefer some people to others. He was not a respecter of persons.

The virtue that would be directed more especially to the poor rather than the rich is not love but compassion. Because the poor are the ones who suffer deprivation and destitution they elicit feelings of compassion in us. To be compassionate is to be moved by the pain and sufferings of others.[13] Important as this is in itself, it is not what is being referred to when we speak about taking an option for the poor.

The option for the poor is an option for the *cause* of the poor.[14] It means taking sides against the cause of the rich. It is a choice related to the unjust economic structures in which we live. It has nothing to do with the moral worth or guilt of any individual poor person or individual wealthy person. Poor people can be personally good, bad, or indifferent. They can be honest or dishonest. But their cause as the victims of oppression and injustice is right.

Poverty is a structural problem. It is one of the consequences of an unjust and sinful economic system. The poor are the victims of sin—whether we are referring to material or formal

[13] Albert Nolan, *Jesus before Christianity*, 25th anniversary ed. (Maryknoll, N.Y.: Orbis Books, 2001), 34–36.
[14] Donal Dorr, *Option for the Poor: A Hundred Years of Catholic Social Teaching*, rev. ed. (Maryknoll, N.Y.: Orbis Books, 1992), 2–3.

sin. They are the ones who are sinned against. The economic structures discriminate against them. Those who want to change this will side with the poor, and the poor themselves will have to take up their own cause. The option for the poor is an option that both the rich and the poor are challenged to make.

One's structural position in a society can influence how one thinks and acts. Rich people are more likely to put their trust in money, while those who have nothing look for security elsewhere. The wealthy are more easily tempted to become greedy. The poor are more likely to rise up against the system that oppresses them than those who benefit from it. The influence of one's position within the structures becomes obvious when we see what happens to poor people who become rich and take on all the usual attitudes of the rich, and rich people who become poor and then suddenly act in ways that are more typical of the poor.

But anyone can come to recognize that the whole structure is unjust and needs to be changed. Both the rich and the poor need to be conscienticized and as a result to take an option for the poor, which is to say, to opt for justice.

Compassion can be a very important element in any action in favor of the poor. But it only becomes an option for the poor once we become aware that poverty is a structural problem.

What we have been exploring here is but one example of the structures of sin: an economically unjust structure. There are others. Patriarchy, for example, is an unjust and sinful structure. In this case we are being called upon to take an option for the rights of women.

Imperialism is another unjust structure. When one nation dominates and dictates to all other nations or many other nations, we can recognize that these power relations are unjust. The Hebrews and Israelites protested loudly against the empires one after the other that oppressed and crushed them. Our option here would be to side with the oppressed nations in any empire. Imperial structures, like the present structure of the United States in relation to the rest of the world, are also structures of sin.

Alternative Structures

Taking an option for the poor is not enough. If we are serious about promoting social justice we need to be taking the next step, which is to contribute as far as we can toward alternative structures, structures that are just and fair. The opposite of structures of sin have sometimes been called "structures of grace." In *SRS*, John Paul II does not make use of this phrase, but what he does refer to as the opposite of structures of sin is "solidarity" (38–40). Solidarity, however, would need to be structured. What would such structures look like?

At the World Food Summit in 1996, *Cor Unum,* the Pontifical Council for Christian and Human Development, described the alternative as "structures of the common good":

> There are many large-scale "structures of sin" which deliberately steer the goods of the earth from their true purpose, that of serving the good of all. . . .
>
> "Cultures of the Common Good" should create means of production of goods and services which have a truly social purpose and promote the common good and not only the private economic benefit of the few and share with the deprived. . . . The obverse of the "structures of sin" are the "structures and cultures of the common good."

SRS describes the virtue of solidarity as "a firm and persevering determination to commit oneself to the common good" (38). There is a long Catholic tradition that presents the common good as the opposite of the unjust pursuit of selfish ends. It is the pursuit of what is best for everyone rather than what is perceived to be best for the individual or the few.

I say "perceived to be" advisedly because in fact there is no contradiction between what is best for the individual or what is best for everyone. The common good is precisely what is best for all of us.

The kind of social structures that people of goodwill and especially Christians would want to work for, then, would be structures that benefit and promote the common good. They would be structures of solidarity and sharing where nobody would be permitted to hoard the goods of the earth while others are deprived of basic needs.

Such structures appear to be a far cry from anything we have at present. They seem like an impossible dream that will only be realized when the kingdom of God appears among us. But that was not how Jesus saw it.

Jesus worked against the structures of his time—structures that encouraged the greed and selfishness of the rich and led to the suffering of the poor—by building small sharing communities.[15] At first this took the form of shared meals. Jesus gathered his followers around the table of fellowship and the sharing of bread. He and his closest disciples shared a common purse that Judas was responsible for, we are told. Luke then presents us with the ideal the early believers strove for in Jerusalem.

> Now the whole group of those who believed were of one heart and soul, and no one claimed private ownership of any possessions, but everything they owned was held in common. . . . There was not a needy person among them, for as many as owned land or houses sold them and brought the proceeds of what was sold. They laid it at the apostles' feet and it was distributed to each as any had need.[16]

---

[15]Nolan, *Jesus Today*, 165–66.
[16]Acts 4:32, 34, 35 (NRSV).

What we have here is an alternative structure, a structure that served the common good of those involved, a structure of solidarity and sharing.[17] It was not easy to maintain. The house churches seem to have made some attempt to share at least at the agape meal, and Paul was operating out of the same principle when he organized his famous collection for the poorer churches.[18] The ideal was kept alive in the traditions of religious life.

The first Christian communities brought together as equals not only the rich and the poor, the well-off and the needy, but also people of different cultures, races, languages, religious backgrounds, genders, and social strata.[19] These communities or churches were alternative social structures. The believers came together as equals, as brothers and sisters, because, as Paul says, "There is no longer Jew or Greek, there is no longer slave or free, there is no longer male or female, for all of you are one in Christ."[20]

The early church communities were more than alternative social structures. But for our purposes here we need to note that they *were* alternative structures that enabled people to think and act independently of the dominant structures.[21] They provided an atmosphere and environment of love, justice, equality, solidarity, and sharing that made it possible to stand up to the structures of sin. In that sense we could call them structures of grace.

A Change of Heart

The introduction of terminology like "structures of sin" into the vocabulary of the social teaching of the church encourages

---

[17]Wes Howard-Brook, *The Church before Christianity* (Maryknoll, N.Y.: Orbis Books, 2001), 95–101.

[18]Rom. 15:25–27; 1 Cor. 16:1–3.

[19]Howard-Brook, *Church before Christianity*, 77–80.

[20]Gal. 3:28 (NRSV).

[21]Howard-Brook, *Church before Christianity*, 98–99.

us to think more structurally about the moral evils of our time. It encourages us to make more effective use of sociology and social theories, and it enables us to do this without losing sight of personal sin and the need for a change of heart—a personal conversion or what we generally call repentance.

Personal conversion from sin and selfishness will not lead to structural change, even if large numbers of people are involved, unless they become aware of the role of structures in the perpetuation of evil, unless they are conscienticized and take an option for the poor and oppressed of all kinds.

On the other hand, a change from structures of sin to structures of grace cannot happen fully and sustainably without personal conversion from sin and selfishness. In South Africa the structures of apartheid were dismantled and replaced by admirable structures of democracy and equality enshrined in a remarkable constitution. But too many of the people involved have not experienced a personal conversion and are now caught up in the unjust structures of the economy that we share with the rest of the world. We have a measure of social liberation, but we do not yet have enough personal liberation.[22]

The personal task of transforming our lives, with God's grace, from selfishness and sin to love and compassion remains as crucial as ever.

---

[22]Nolan, *Jesus Today*, xiii.

Selected Bibliography of Albert Nolan's Work

1976

1976. *Jesus before Christianity*. Cape Town: David Philip (1977, London: Darton, Longman, and Todd; 1978, Maryknoll, N.Y.: Orbis Books).

1982

1982a. "South Africa: Social Analysis, Part I: The Dominant Ideology in South Africa Today." *Grace and Truth* 3, no. 1: 33–46.

1982b. "South Africa: Social Analysis, Part II: Resistance to the Dominant Ideology." *Grace and Truth* 3, no. 2: 84–93.

1982c. "The Political and Social Context." In *Catholics in Apartheid Society*, edited by A. Prior, 1–21. Cape Town: David Philip.

1984

1984a. "Evangelization and Human Liberation." *Grace and Truth* 5, no. 4: 158–66.

1984b. "Justice in the Bible." In *Justice and Truth Shall Meet*, edited by P. Wood, 74–85. Conference Proceedings, Sinsinawa, Wisc. *Parable*.

1985

1985a. *Taking Sides*. London: Catholic Truth Society.

1985b. "The Option of the Poor in South Africa." In *Resistance and Hope: South African Essays in Honor of Beyers Naudé*, edited by Charles Villa-Vicencio and John de Gruchy, 189-98. Cape Town: David Philip.

1985c. *The Service of the Poor and Spiritual Growth*. London: Catholic Institute for International Relations.

1986

1986a. *Academic Freedom: A Service to the People.* T. D. Davie Memorial Lecture. Cape Town: UCT.

1986b. *Biblical Spirituality.* Johannesburg: Order of Preachers.

1986c. "Spiritual Growth and the Option for the Poor." *Dominican Ashram 5*, no. 3: 107–14.

1986d. "Theology in a Prophetic Mode." In *Hammering Swords into Ploughshares: Essays in Honor of Archbishop Mpilo Desmond Tutu*, edited by B. Tlhagale and I. Mosala, 131–40. Grand Rapids: William B. Eerdmans.

1986e. "The Option of the Poor in South Africa." *New Blackfriars* 67: 787.

1987

1987a. "The Legitimacy and Illegitimacy of the State." *Grace and Truth 8*, no. 2: 91–96.

1987b. "Lectures on the Theology of Liberation." In A. Nolan and R. Broderick, *To Nourish Our Faith: The Theology of Liberation in South Africa.* Hilton: Order of Preachers.

1987c. "The Eschatology of the Kairos Document." *Missionalia 15*, no. 2: 61-69.

1988

1988. *God in South Africa: The Challenge of the Gospel.* Capetown: David Philip (London: CIIR; Grand Rapids: William B. Eerdmans).

1989

1989. "The Bible and the Struggle for Democracy." Address delivered at the Diakonia Democracy Conference, August 1989.

1990

1990. "The Paradigm Shift." *Grace and Truth 10*, no. 2: 97–103.

1991

1991a. "Evangelism, Mission and Evangelisation." Johannesburg: CPSA (in *Grapevine: Papers on Ministry and Mission*, no. 30).

1991b. "Conflict and Community." In *Becoming a Creative Local Church*, edited by Patrick Hartin, Paul Decock, and Bernard Connor, 172-83. Pietermaritzburg: Cluster Publications.

1991c. "Economic Justice." In *Christianity and Democracy: Lenten*

Lectures, 36–40. Johannesburg and Cape Town: Justice and Peace Commissions.

1991d. "Poor in Spirit." *Readings in Redemptorist Spirituality* 5: 176–86.

1991e. "Doing Theology in the South African Context." In *Trends in Mission: Toward the Third Millennium*, edited by William Jenkinson and Helene O'Sullivan, 235–38. Maryknoll, N.Y.: Orbis Books.

1994

1994. "Kairos Theology." In *Doing Theology in Context: South African Perspectives*, edited by John W. de Gruchy and Charles Villa-Vicencio, 212–18. Maryknoll, N.Y.: Orbis Books.

1995

1995a. "What Is Contextual Theology? A South African Perspective." In *Upptackter I kontexten: Teologiska till minne av per Frostin*, edited by Sigurd Bergmann and Goran Eidevall, 10–19. Lund: Institutet for kontextuell teologi.

1995b. "Church and State in a Changing Context." In *Being the Church in South Africa Today*, edited by Barney Pityana and Charles Villa-Vicencio, 151–56. Johannesburg: South African Council of Churches.

1996

1996. "Work, the Bible, Workers and Theologians: Elements of a Workers' Theology." *Semeia* 73: 213–20. Previously published in James Cochrane and Gerald West, eds. *The Threefold Cord: Theology, Work and Labour*. Pietermaritzburg: Cluster Publications.

1999

1999. "Eles me chamam de comunista." In *Helder, O Dom: Uma vida que marcou os rumos da igreja no Brasil*, edited by Zildo Rocha, 53–55. Petropolis: Editora Vozes.

2004

2004. "Reconciliation: The South African Perspective." *Priests and People* 18, no. 3: 92–97.

2005

2005. "Albert Nolan." In *Building Bridges: Dominicans Doing Theol-*

ogy Together, edited by Dominican Sisters International, 129–32. Dublin: Dominican Publications.

2006
2006a. "Preaching and Contemplation." In *The Grace and Task of Preaching*, edited by Michael Monshau, 238–54. Dublin: Dominican Publications.
2006b. *Jesus Today: A Spirituality of Radical Freedom*. Maryknoll, N.Y.: Orbis Books.

2007
2007a. "The Oikos Journey: A New Kairos Document." *Challenge: Church and People* 86: 10–11.
2007b. "The Art of Teaching Theology." In *Toward the Intelligent Use of Liberty: Dominican Approaches in Education*, edited by Gabrielle Kelly and Kevin Saunders, 135–42. Adelaide, Australia: ATP Press.
2007c. "Structures of Sin." *Angelicum* 84: 625–37.

2009
2009. "Hope in an Age of Despair." *International Dominican Information* 468: 12–15.

Index